A TERRIBLE BEAUTY

A TERRIBLE BEAUTY

The Fierce Splendour of Gospel
and Grace

Chick Yuill

MILTON KEYNES ● COLORADO SPRINGS
● HYDERABAD

Equipping the Church for action

14 13 12 11 10 09 08   7 6 5 4 3 2 1

First published 2008 by Spring Harvest Publishing Division and
Authentic Media
9 Holdom Avenue, Bletchley, Milton Keynes, MK1 1QR, UK
1820 Jet Stream Drive, Colorado Springs, CPO 80921, USAOM
Authentic Media, Medchal Road, Jeedimetla Village,
Secunderabad 500 055, A.P., India
www.authenticmedia.co.uk
Authentic Media is a division of IBS-STL U.K., limited by
guarantee, with its Registered Office at Kingstown Broadway,
Carlisle, Cumbria CA3 0HA. Registered in England & Wales No.
1216232. Registered charity 270162

British Library Cataloguing in Publication Data

A catalogue record for this book is available from the
British Library

ISBN: 978-1-85078-796-9

Cover Design by fourninezero design.
Print Management by Adare
Printed in Great Britain by J.H. Haynes & Co., Sparkford

for
my wonderful wife
who unhesitatingly walked with me into an
uncertain future

and my faithful friends
whose prayers and support transformed a
desert experience ino a fertile place of liberty
and creativity

contents

foreword

For centuries the Church has been the caretaker of truth, goodness and beauty. However, for some of us in the Protestant West, beauty has become the Cinderella of this particular trinity. While God's truth is trumpeted by our proclamation of the gospel and his goodness shouted aloud in our ministry, beauty often sits quietly by. On a practical note, the aesthetic has often been forgotten in every day church life. Some of us, who have holidayed abroad and stood in awe of Catholic and Orthodox architecture, have wondered why our chapels and churches appear so drab in comparison. And yet, as this book reminds us, truth, goodness and beauty are equally essential parts of church life. More importantly, in the gospel they are interdependent realities. Put simply, the gospel is always beautiful, good and true.

There are many reasons for the relegation of beauty in the Protestant church, not least the Reformation, when church leaders were quick to challenge idolatry and quicker still to call Christians to worship Christ rather than the objects and artefacts that portrayed him. That aside, for some, the notion that beauty has an equal footing with truth and goodness is problematic. After all, while every aspect of the gospel can be seen as true and good, can the same be said of beauty? Take the crucifixion. Although truth and goodness abound on Calvary's hillside, beauty seems strangely absent from the execution of God's Son. If anything, this day is the objectification of all ugliness. How could these events ever be regarded as beautiful?

As Chick points out, the events of that first Easter have a beauty all their own; albeit a terrible beauty, a beauty which is entirely uncomfortable yet eternally comforting. Here, in the aftermath of the crucifixion, we find ourselves sickened and healed, guilty yet forgiven, judged and saved. But how might we explain Calvary's terrible beauty? As theologians have argued throughout the ages, God's beauty transcends our own thoughts and tastes. His beauty is simply higher, wider and deeper than our understanding can allow or disposition dictate. As the beginning of all things God retains the right to blow our minds, challenge our dispositions and surprise us with the sheer size and scope of his beauty. In him, even those things that we previously designated 'ugly' can become party to the beautiful. As the hymn writer writes, 'Those wounds yet visible above in beauty glorified.'

Over two thousand years ago and several centuries before Christ, the prophet Isaiah makes exactly this point (Is. 52:13 – 53:12). Here, in one of the most evocative passages of the Old Testament, Isaiah describes the suffering that God's Servant will undertake in order to bring salvation to his people. He will not be good-looking or gorgeous, stunning or striking, at least in any conventional way. Far from staring into his eyes, people will hide their faces from him. And yet in his life and death God's people will find their forgiveness and freedom, their hope and salvation. These ancient verses enabled the Church to identify Jesus as the Messiah and helped his followers to make sense of his life, death and resurrection. Later on, Chick will expound this prophecy further. For now, it is enough to point out that the day on which Christ was marred and deformed beyond human likeness, marked the moment when he saved the world. On this day and that hillside, the arrested, tortured, crucified and executed Jesus was crowned as the King of the Jews and servant of all. In the ugly scenes of Good Friday we somehow glimpse the vivid spectrum of God's beauty.

Two thousand years later, Chick eloquently explores this terrible beauty. Asking searching questions and probing the deepest of mysteries, Chick encourages us that God's beauty is there to be found in the pain and the problems of our earthly life and human condition. To discover God in fullness is not to retreat from the mess of the world but to embrace the beauty of a cursed creation; to roll up our sleeves and fall to our knees; to dig deep and offer all that we unearth in prayer and penitence. If we have courage enough to do this we will surely discover that God's beauty can stretch to cover our flawed and imperfect lives. As Chick so powerfully points out, we too can be beautified by the resurrected Christ.

To write the foreword for a book as wonderful as this is an honour. However it is an even greater privilege to count the author as a friend. Chick and Margaret Yuill are both my friends and my heroes. Journeying with them these past years has provided me with a firsthand insight into the life-changing content of these pages. It's as if, having seen the movie, I'm now reading the book. As a result, I am so glad that others will now be able to share in their remarkable adventure. The telling truths and inspiring insights to come are derived from deep theological reflection and powerful personal experience.

The wisdom and revelation herein are not simply the stuff of reading and learning but come from sacrificial living and costly faithfulness. In short, the battles and victories of *A Terrible Beauty* have been hard fought and hard won, well in advance of its publication. For Chick and Margaret, God's beauty has saved the day and created a new way.

Of all the scenes in movie history, the closing moments of one of Hollywood's earliest epics stands out. In the aftermath of a final battle, we are left to ponder King Kong's final demise. A policeman turns to Carl Denham and says, 'The airplanes got him.' Denham replies, 'Oh no, it wasn't the airplanes. It was beauty [that] killed the beast.' In this, the movie's lead recognises what Christian theologians and thinkers such as Chick Yuill have long since recognised, namely that beauty will save the world.

Russell Rook
(February 2008 London)

prologue

The Irish poet, William Butler Yeats, had little respect for a group of his peers and acquaintances who had espoused the cause of Irish nationalism in the first couple of decades of the twentieth century. His conversations with them amounted only to 'polite meaningless words' and, in his eyes, they were little more than jesters who 'lived where motley is worn', play-actors performing their pointless and pretentious roles in what he perceived to be 'the casual comedy' of their lives.

But his opinions were to be dramatically overturned by the events of the Easter Rising, an armed insurrection in the spring of 1916 against British rule in Ireland. Far from being mere play-acting, as Yeats had thought, this was all too serious. Violence erupted and blood ran freely in the streets of Dublin as the British forces acted swiftly and ruthlessly to crush the rebellion. Not long afterwards, fifteen of the leaders – some of whom were the very people Yeats had so glibly dismissed – were executed for their part in the uprising.

Yeats' poem *Easter 1916* is his tribute to his fallen friends and his witness to the new state of affairs their deaths have ushered in. Rooted in the culture of Ireland

and in the events of the time, it has, nonetheless, like all great art, a wider application than the immediate circumstances which inspired its creation. It is a powerful and eloquent testimony to what happens when fierce reality breaks through mere rhetoric, when cosy sentimentality is overtaken by costly sacrifice.

There is a recurring refrain running through the verses which comes as close as words ever can to expressing the profound mystery and the perplexing mixture of agony and ecstasy which are laid bare by such events

> All changed, changed utterly:
> A terrible beauty is born.

And the title of the poem is more than simply a reference to the date of the uprising. Attentive readers cannot help but notice, whatever their take on Irish history and politics, that behind the story of this particular act of sacrifice for political and patriotic convictions lie the greater events of the first Easter which changed the world radically and for ever. The image of the man on the cross is both terrible and beautiful in equal measure. Once you have seen it for what it is, your world can never be the same again.

It is to that 'terrible beauty' that this book will seek to direct your attention; a fierce splendour that is shot through human experience and which we all must encounter and even embrace if we are to experience life in all its fullness.

One

personal: going to Jerusalem

I don't do altar calls.

What I mean is, I don't normally *respond* to them. It may be a deep-seated shyness; it may be a fear of being manipulated; it may be my typically Scottish reluctance to demonstrate deep emotion in public; or it may simply be that, having spent over thirty years of my life in a part of the church that ends almost every act of public worship with an opportunity and appeal to those present to 'step forward and kneel at the mercy seat' and having issued the call so often myself, I've become hardened or even immune to any pressure to get up out of my seat and walk to the front.

The point is – I really need to make this clear – I don't do altar calls.

Which is why you need to know how I came to be the first person standing at the front in Elmwood Church in Salford on a Monday in June 2005. To be honest, I'm still not entirely sure myself. I hadn't even intended to be there. I'd been at a denominational conference for most of the previous week, work had piled up and I just didn't think I could take any more time out of the office. But Debra, who had organised the day for leaders in the north west of England, called me on the morning of the event to ask if I'd share the leadership with her and stand in for her husband Frank, who had to spend the day at the hospital with their son who'd broken his ankle playing football. Anxious to be helpful, I told her that I'd come just for the morning, thinking that I'd slip off at lunchtime and head back to the office.

The problem was that the speaker was particularly on form that day. I'd heard him on numerous occasions previously and always enjoyed his ability to combine laughter and tears with wonderfully relevant Bible teaching. But that day was different. The laughter had a particularly therapeutic quality and the assembled church leaders were all aware, I think, of something unusually wholesome and healing in the worship and teaching.

And that's really why I decided to forget the stuff back at the office and stay for the afternoon. The previous week had been a particularly tough one. There had been an incident at the conference which had proved to be extremely painful, which had caused me to feel under personal attack, and which had brought into sharp focus a number of issues with which I had been struggling. I knew deep in my heart that I would have to respond, though I was unsure how to do that or even whether I would have the courage to do so. I needed something – some kind of guidance, or healing, or both. And the solid teaching and strong fellowship I was enjoying were certainly doing me more good than a day in the office.

Which brings us back to the altar call.

That afternoon the teaching was based on Paul's farewell to the elders of the Ephesian Church in Acts 20 and the speaker homed in on verses 22–24

And now, compelled by the Spirit, I am going to Jerusalem, not knowing what will happen to me there. I only know that in every city the Holy Spirit warns me that prison and hardships are facing me. However, I consider my life worth nothing to me, if only I may finish the race and complete the task the Lord Jesus has given me – the task of testifying to God's grace.

As he brought his message to a conclusion, the preacher said simply, 'There are some Christian leaders here who know that they have to "go to Jerusalem". There are no guarantees as to how it will all turn out, but you know what God wants you do and you need to do it, whatever the consequences.' Then he invited anyone to step forward who felt the need to respond to this word and who would appreciate prayer. And that's the moment when I 'got up and got out of my seat', the first person to step forward that afternoon. Just how much that moment would change my life, how much it would cost and how much I would learn over the next couple of years, I couldn't even begin to comprehend as I stood at the front of Elmwood Church that day.

The first thing that happened was that I sat down and wrote a letter the next day. Words and writing have always been one of the things that I've done reasonably well, but never have I worked so hard to find the right words and strike the right tone as I did in that letter. Despite my best efforts, I wrote it with a sense of foreboding and a deep conviction that, however sensitively I might manage to balance courtesy and honesty, it might not be well received. I was not wrong! It committed me to a stand on matters of leadership, power and church governance that was to mean that just over a year later I would walk away from ministry and leadership in a denomination where my wife Margaret and I had served for more than thirty years, which had brought my parents to faith, which had nurtured me in the gospel, where many of my closest friends continue to minister and for which I retain a warm affection, a deep respect and a lasting gratitude.

On one level it was the darkest period of my entire life. In the weeks and months following my letter, there was a series of painful meetings in which I tried unsuccessfully to resolve the issues; there was all the hurt of separating myself from something which I had always believed to be a life-time commitment; and there was the uncertainty and unpredictability of the future without a secure job or a regular income. In those days immediately preceding and following my resignation, Margaret and I spent many hours walking and talking, trying to make sense of it all. There was, of course, a great deal of sadness and not a few tears. But there was also light in the darkness – the certainty that we were doing the right thing, the fact that we felt no sense of personal bitterness towards anyone, the support of friends and colleagues from around the world and – more than anything else – the growing sense that God was teaching us things about the mystery of his grace and guidance at a level of our being that we had never before experienced.

There were truths to which I had long assented intellectually and which I had preached to others over the years that I began to understand at a deep and personal level: that it is possible to be deeply saddened without being in any way unhappy; that tears and laughter are close companions; that holding on to the certainty of God's love has to coexist with an awareness that there is an inescapable uncertainty about life itself; that faith involves learning to be a believer in the dark; that there are no guarantees as to how things will turn out; that allowing God to be God means accepting that he will

sometimes be silent – even apparently passive and inac-
tive – when we are almost screaming at him to do something on our behalf. And there was a growing conviction
that I was beginning to apprehend God's love in a new
and deeper way, not simply *in spite of* the hurt but,
rather, *in and through* the pain. It was a little like watching an image on a screen where the focus was becoming
clearer, slowly but surely and the picture that was merg-
ing from the blur was one of an intense beauty, fierce
and terrible, but infinitely more desirable than mere
happiness or personal comfort.

Of course, anyone who is old enough and wise enough
to know anything at all about life will immediately
recognise that, when compared to the pain and trouble
that afflict so many people in this world, what we were
going through was hardly worthy of mention. And I'd be
the first to agree. In the grand scheme of things, in the
scale of world tragedies and personal suffering, our
experience would definitely be right at the bottom of the
table. There are thousands of children dying every day
who have never had the chance of a decent life, there are
millions suffering from HIV and Aids and countless
human beings have their lives blighted by famine, war
and natural disasters. And while we were walking our
particular path, two of our dearest and closest friends, a
married couple with four children, were coming to terms
with the news that the wife had a type of cancer with a
prognosis that, humanly speaking, gave little cause for
hope. So I'm the first to acknowledge that our confrontation with suffering was and is little more than a border
skirmish, when set against the long and costly battles
that so many people face every day.

But, for all that, it was and is real enough. Common
sense will tell you that a splinter under your fingernail
is far less severe than a blow with a sword, but if you've

never experienced pain before, the splinter will be sufficient to introduce you to what it means to be physically
hurt! My experience served as a call to face up to the pain
of life, to re-examine the things I believe and to cut
through so much of the glib words and superficial reli-
giosity that masquerade as real faith. More than anything
else, it caused me to look again at the nature of grace. Like
so many others, I have been greatly impacted by the
renewed emphasis in recent years on the extravagant generosity of grace, the great foundational truth that God
loves us irrespective of anything wrong we might have
done or anything good we might have achieved, and the
long-overdue recognition that grace must not be
restrained in any ecclesiastical system and cannot be con-
tained in any theological framework. All those things are
good and need to be stated again and again.

However, I suspect that grace is much richer, more
complex and much more nuanced than many of our
formulaic doctrinal statements. I don't want you to misunderstand me at this point. I'm definitely not proposing that we should substitute a programme of legalistic
self-discipline for God's free grace or that we should
change the whole agenda and get on to a treadmill of
trying to earn God's favour by our good works. It's not
that at all. What the last year has alerted me to, what I'm
reaching out for, what I'm trying to put into words is
this: to be embraced by grace and to embrace it in return,
is to accept not only that you are accepted and loved by
God, but that you are cooperating in a process of growth
in which every experience has meaning and can become
redemptive.

Those older translations of the Bible that rendered the
famous verse from Paul's Letter to the Romans as 'all
things work together for good to them that love God'
(Rom. 8:28: King James Version) were less than accurate.

That simply isn't true. If it were the case, it would mean that millions who have suffered unjustly have, by definition, been shut out of God's grace. There is no guarantee that things will always work out well. The better translation, however, is 'in all things God work for the good of those who love him' (NIV). Some of those things will be dark and painful, sometimes even terrible, but they will be part of that terrible but transforming beauty that gives purpose and hope to life.

To put it another way, it's grace that changes our lives from being merely a series of events, pleasant or otherwise, to a story – something that has direction and dynamic and meaning. What makes a story worth reading is not that every page is laughter and smiles and that everything runs smoothly. Stories like that are inevitably bland and boring. What makes a story interesting is the development and interaction of characters, the unfolding of the plot with its unexpected twists and turns, the overcoming of obstacles and the gradual emergence of some kind of ultimate pattern and purpose in the narrative.

And every personal story is played out against a backdrop of larger events, the great movements of history and culture that provide the context for each individual life. Grace is much more than the love and favour of God to individual people. It is on a larger scale the backdrop to our lives, the great movement and impetus of the unfolding purposes of God for his entire creation with which our lives are linked. We are like Frodo in *The Lord of the Rings* who is caught up in events far larger than himself or the normal happenings of the Shire where he lives with his fellow hobbits, drawn into adventures that he could never have imagined. We, too, are caught up in the magnificent, sweeping movement of grace. God's great redemptive plan for creation is being worked out *within* us: what he does in each one of us – renewing what has been marred and obscured by sin, painstakingly restoring his perfect image in us – is in microcosm what he will one day do for his entire creation. But it is also being worked out *through* us: each individual story is vital to the larger story. There is a part for each of us to play in his great unfolding plan of redemption. It may not be a starring role, it may be costly and painful at times, it may seem to be of little consequence when seen close up, but it does have purpose and it does have ultimate meaning.

The story is still unfinished, the great denouement has not yet been reached, the climax is still to come. But the story continues. There will certainly be pleasant fertile valleys ahead of us where we can relax and be refreshed, but there will also be mountains to climb and dangerous paths to negotiate where accidents will happen, blows will be received and scars will remain. We will not be left unmarked or unchanged. But that's the whole point of the journey – that we might be changed utterly and that a terrible beauty might be brought to birth in us.

Two

passion: looking at Calvary

I'm constantly insisting to sceptical visitors that the weather in Manchester really isn't any worse than anywhere else in England. But even I had to admit that it was one of those raw and rainy evenings for which the city is notorious. The very thought of answering the knock at the door on such a night was enough to make me turn up the central heating a couple of degrees as I came downstairs. The young woman who stood there was in her early twenties, I guessed, though the upturned hood of her jacket and the scarf wrapped around her face made it difficult to be sure. It was easier to identify her accent, which was definitely eastern European, but her English was good and she told me that she was Polish and studying at one of the universities in the city.

Before I could respond, she opened a large black portfolio and asked if I would buy one of her drawings. The money, she explained, would help her fund her studies. Since none of the drawings was to my artistic taste and since our evening meal was just about to go on the table, I promptly declined the opportunity to make a purchase. There was just a hint of desperation in her voice when she countered with the suggestion that they'd make great Christmas presents. It was at that point that my well-developed sense of resistance to over-persistent sales people kicked in. If I didn't actually say 'Thanks, but no thanks', that was certainly the gist of my curt response as I closed the door.

My distinct and sudden lack of appetite as I sat down to eat and the strength of my emotions as I reflected on what had just happened took me by surprise. I felt ashamed at my reaction. I've got two daughters of my own, both of whom went through university some years ago, one of whom now lives six thousand miles away from us. The thought that someone would treat them with the same lack of compassion that I'd just shown to the young Polish girl on my door-step was enough to bring tears to my eyes. I quickly grabbed some money, waited until she came back up the street, (having experienced, I guessed, the same reaction from most of my neighbours as she'd had from me) called her back and told her that I really would like to buy one of her drawings. There was a poignant moment when she smiled at me with a mixture of gratitude and embarrassment before she took my money, gave me the picture and headed off into the night.

That brief door-step encounter has stuck in my mind. Why did I feel so bad, why did I have to put it right and why did I sleep so much easier that night because of what I'd done? My action certainly doesn't qualify as an act of heroism; I hadn't done anything brave or risked my life to save someone. And you'd be hard pushed to describe it as a demonstration of holiness; it felt like the very least I could have done. As I've reflected on it, I've been driven to the conclusion that what I did that evening – and what I almost failed to do – was nothing more or less than an expression of basic humanity. I had done what millions of people do every day: I had empathised with someone else, put myself in their place, embraced something of their pain and tried to do something about it. I had simply behaved like a human being.

To be human surely means much more than to eat, sleep, procreate and take care of ourselves and our families. Animals do no less than that. True humanity demands that we recognise that the world is magnificent but marred, that all around us and deep within us there is abundant evidence of generosity and greed, hope and despair, joy and misery, health and sickness, love and loneliness, light and darkness – all co-existing in the paradox of life. To act with humanity is to break free from the narrow confines of our own lives and our own interests, to reach for all that is good and positive, to stand against whatever is wrong and to enter into the hurts of others with help and healing. People of all faiths and none recognise those things in their better moments.

Of course, the opposite is equally true about human beings. We are often less than truly human. Our ability to choose light over darkness, to care for others before self, is matched and often surpassed by our capacity for selfishness and depravity. Too much of the history of nations is a dark litany of war, cruelty and bloodshed; and our individual stories contain too many moments of petty jealousies, hurts inflicted on others and unhealed bitterness. Our inhumanity touches everything and everyone. We hardly need the ancient and profound Genesis story of the Fall to tell us that the entire creation is infected by our moral and spiritual sickness. The ecological damage that our selfish and careless pillaging of finite resources has inflicted on our fragile planet is sufficient testimony to that truth.

But what if my troubled conscience and my subsequent actions that cold night in Manchester really are a pointer to the truth that our humanity, at its very best, is created to put service before self, to choose light rather than darkness, to enter into and share the pain of a fellow human being? What if self-giving love really does lie at the very heart of what God means us to be? And what if the world were to see someone who *perfectly* embodied our humanity and who *fully* embraced the pain and the hurt of others? Such a person would carry an overwhelming – one might even say intolerable – burden for the rest of humankind, would inevitably be misunderstood by many, would in some terrible way bear the sins of the world.

I am not the first to reflect on those questions by any means. Centuries before Christ, the poet-prophet Isaiah pondered the mystery of one who would be the perfect servant of God and humanity. His words are a testimony to a beauty so wonderful and terrible that we can hardly bear to look at it.

> He grew up before him like a tender shoot,
> and like a root out of dry ground.
> He had no beauty or majesty to attract us to him,
> nothing in his appearance that we should desire him.
> He was despised and rejected by men,
> a man of sorrows, and familiar with suffering.
> Like one from whom men hide their faces
> he was despised and we esteemed him not.
> Surely he took up our infirmities
> and carried our sorrows,
> yet we considered him stricken by God,
> smitten by him, and afflicted.
> But he was pierced for our transgressions,
> he was crushed for our iniquities;
> the punishment that brought us peace was upon him,
> and by his wounds we are healed.

We all, like sheep, have gone astray,
and each of us has turned to his own way;
and the LORD has laid on him
the iniquity of us all.

(Isa. 53:2–6).

This is nothing less than a word-picture of perfect humanity. Of course, it is the conviction of Christians across the centuries that Isaiah's prophetic poem is more than just a dream, that it has found its fulfilment in the life and death of the man, Jesus from Nazareth. Such is the impact of that life and such is our sense of awe and wonder as we look at Jesus, that the Christian Church has rightly and inevitably been driven to the conclusion that, in Jesus, humanity and divinity have been united, that Jesus is truly the Son of God, that such a life is possible only because God has chosen to become human in Jesus. And it is only when we hold tightly to the seemingly contradictory truth of the divinity and the humanity of Jesus, refusing to let go of either aspect of his being, that we can begin to grasp the wonder of the cross and come to terms with a vital aspect of New Testament teaching that puzzles and troubles many sensitive believers: *Why should the only truly good man who ever lived have to go through the agony of crucifixion? Surely God could have declared his love for us and offered his forgiveness to the world without such pain and suffering?*

One answer is simply to say that the ways of God are so far above our puny minds that this is a mystery that we can never fully understand and to some extent that is true. But it is also true to say that God is a God who chooses to reveal himself to us and who invites us to know him and to understand his ways and his work. And, if we come to the New Testament with both head and heart, both intellect and imagination, we will certainly glimpse the fierce

splendour of gospel and grace in the cross. In his first letter to the church at Thessalonica, Paul tells his readers that
it is the death of Jesus that 'delivers us from the coming
wrath' (Thes. 1:10). In so doing, he is reminding them of a
concept that occurs again and again in the New Testament;
a holy God who has created a moral universe cannot simply ignore our sin, and the entire human race stands under
his judgement. But on the cross Jesus has paid the penalty
and taken all the pain of our sin. He has died for us. So
how can we reconcile the concept of an angry Father pun-
ishing his innocent Son for something he didn't do with
the fact that he is a God of love? I want to suggest that
there are three directions from which we can approach the
cross that will enable us to see its terrible beauty and to
worship and wonder in the presence of the One who lived
for others and who died for us.

Partners

It would be impossible to look at the cross and describe
it as a pretty or a pleasing sight. Crucifixion was one of
the most horrific forms of capital punishment ever
devised. After being viciously beaten, the victim was
often made to carry the cross-beam through the streets as
a warning to others who might think of transgressing
Roman law. At the place of execution, the cross would be
set on the ground and the victim would be laid on it,
their hands pinned to the cross beam by rough nails. A
saddle halfway up the upright beam would allow the
body some rest – not for their comfort, but only to ensure
that the weight of the body didn't cause the nails to rip
right through the hands. Death could take a long time,
wounds would fester, breathing was all but impossible,
circulation was severely restricted, thirst was unbearable

and the pain was excruciating. It was sickening enough when inflicted on criminals who had broken the law. In the case of Jesus, who had done nothing wrong, who had been tried by a court acting illegally and found guilty on trumped-up charges, it was hideously unjust.

When you ask why it should have happened to Jesus, the answer is simple enough on one level. A man who would live for others, who would make it his business to embrace the outcast and the marginalized, who would offer a love that could not be constrained by any religious system, who would stand against vested interests, even and especially when they were done in the name of a religion – a man like that would inevitably have powerful enemies. And Jesus had disturbed many powerful people, particularly those who had believed that they had cornered the market on God. It's not too difficult to see why they wanted him out of the way and why they would go to any lengths to be rid of him. But behind the history and the facts that can be investigated there lies a mystery, a deeper level of truth that is discernible only to those who approach the cross with the eyes of faith.

For terrible as his death was in its inhumanity and injustice, there is also a beauty about the death of Jesus which has fascinated and drawn generations of painters, poets and musicians. Albert Orsborn's somewhat sentimental gospel song captures that strange attraction of the figure of the dying man just as well as many works of arguably greater artistic merit

> Many thoughts stir my heart as I ponder alone;
> Many places attract me with charms all their own;
> But the thought of all thoughts is of Christ crucified,
> The place of all places, the hill where he died.
> O the charm of the cross! How I love to be there!
> With the love that shines from it, what love can compare?

It is Isaiah's poem that awakens us to the reason for this attraction. When we look at the cross we are seeing humanity at its glorious best, humanity as God wants it to be. Jesus is the fulfilment of Isaiah's dream – the truly human one, the one whose life is perfectly open to God, the one who deliberately faces darkness and evil, the one who carries the pain of others, a willing victim bearing the sins and hurts of the world. *But the beauty goes still deeper*. For the one who dies on the cross is, as we have acknowledged, God incarnate, God come amongst us in frail humanity. It is impossible to articulate the Christian doctrine of the Trinity – Father, Son and Spirit in eternal, perfect fellowship – with the precision of a mathematical formula. It will always be beyond the boundaries of our understanding, but it is the only satisfactory way we can describe the self-revelation of God through his dealings with his people Israel, through the life and death of Jesus and through the Church's experience of his abiding and empowering presence in the Holy Spirit.

But some things we can and must say with certainty. And one of those things is that the Father and the Son can never be set at odds. The truth of the Trinity – a God who lives in perfect, loving, fellowship – will not permit us to see the cross *exclusively* as the action of a righteous, wrathful Judge on the one side and the offering of a loving Saviour on the other side, though that image will certainly help us to understand the horror of human sin, the offence it causes to a holy God and the extent of Jesus' sacrificial offering for us. But it is not enough to say that Jesus died on the cross to satisfy the wrath of an angry Father *and to leave it at that*. We also need to understand that he came, as John's great précis of the gospel makes clear, not primarily because God was angry, but because 'God so loved the world that he gave his one and only Son' (Jn. 3:16). His death was not just an expression of righteous anger, but also the supreme example of a rescue act that encompasses all humanity and the entire creation. To quote John's words further: 'God did not send his Son into the world to condemn the world, but to save the world through him' (Jn. 3:17). As if to put the matter beyond any possible doubt, Paul pushes the truth even further when he writes, with a confidence that must have been startling to his first readers, for whom crucifixion was the ultimate humiliation, that 'God was in reconciling the world to himself in Christ' (2 Cor. 5:19).

To come at it from another angle, when the New Testament wants to describe God in one word, it does it by stating simply that 'God is *love*' (I Jn. 4:8). It never defines him in the phrase 'God is *wrath.*' That is not to say that a righteous and holy wrath is not part of God's character, but it is to say that his wrath, his anger, is an aspect of his love. (It's a truth we understand on the purely human level; as a father I was sometimes angry with my children, not because I had stopped loving them, or even in spite of my love for them, but precisely *because I loved them.* I wanted the best for them and hated to see them taking a wrong course of action.) The wonder of Calvary is that on the cross these two things – God's infinite love and his righteous anger – come together perfectly. Here is the miracle of the cross: *God not only exacts the penalty for our sin; in his Son Jesus he pays that penalty on our behalf!* Rather than the cross being exclusively the place of divine punishment, it is actually the scene of a reconciling partnership – a partnership not only between Father and Son in the Godhead, but a partnership between God and humanity, a partnership between a loving God and the only perfectly willing and obedient man who ever lived. The pain of the cross is

terrible in the fullest sense of that word; but the partnership transforms a place of brutality into a scene of inde-
scribable beauty.

Pictures

The second direction from which we need to approach
the cross involves a recognition of the way in which the
New Testament writers seek to express the meaning and
the wonder of what had happened at Calvary and of the
difference it had made to life. The New Testament is not
a book of systematic theology in which doctrinal themes
are followed through analytically. Rather it is a testimony
to a new reality that had broken in upon the earliest
believers through the life, death and resurrection of Jesus,
a reality that they are passionately seeking to share with
all who will listen. Of course, they come back to the subject of the cross again and again, they come at it from
many different angles and they describe it in different
ways. But there is a dynamic about all that they say, a
sense that what they are speaking of is ultimately beyond
the scope of language, an understanding that the best
their words can be is a window that will allow men and
women to witness and experience a truth that goes
beyond what can be grasped by intellect alone. Heart and
head must work together if we are to reach out in faith to
what God has done in Jesus.

The practice of explaining the cross by reference to
'theories of the atonement' as is all too often the case in
doctrinal manuals and theological colleges, would probably have amazed – and surely dismayed – the New
Testament writers. What had happened was far too
wonderful to be reduced to a theory. They were not
offering doctrinal propositions to satisfy the intellect;

they were painting dramatic word pictures to capture the imagination and awaken faith, word pictures which not only linked the terrible events of the cross to the transforming experience they now enjoyed, but which resonated with the culture of the communities in which they lived and with whom they were anxious to share their good news. There were two pictures that particularly caught their imagination.

Those early believers discovered very quickly that they had a new liberty through their relationship to the crucified and risen Christ. The old life of religious observance, of moral failure, of spiritual hunger, of judgement and condemnation – all that seemed like a kind of slavery compared to the experience of forgiveness and acceptance they now enjoyed. And it was all because of what Jesus had done; their new-found freedom had come about at the cost of his life and death. He had set them free and done for them what they knew they could never have achieved by their own efforts. So what could be more natural than that they should echo Jesus' own words (Mk. 10:45) and speak of his death as a ransom price that had set them free? In a world where slavery was at the heart of the economic system and where criminal and political kidnappings were almost daily occurrences, what picture could be more easily understood and what would be more appealing? In addition, for Jewish people the idea of a God who redeems and rescues his people out of slavery had an added resonance as they remembered and celebrated how God had acted to liberate them from slavery in Egypt. Little wonder that the idea of the cross as a ransom runs right through the New Testament.

The other great picture used in the writings and preaching of the Early Church was that of sacrifice. It was an obvious image for the first followers of Jesus, nurtured as they had been in orthodox Judaism, in which animal sacrifice lay at the very foundation of their faith and practice. It is easy for us to misunderstand sacrifice as nothing more than a bloodthirsty way of appeasing an angry God. But that is not how it was seen by God-fearing Jews. For them, sacrifice was God's gracious provision, a dramatic and symbolic way in which sinful people could bridge the gulf that their sin had caused between them and God. Every Jew believed that the life of any creature was in its blood and that that life belonged only to God. That's why Jewish dietary regulations forbade eating the blood of any animal. So when the blood of the animal was poured out on the altar, the priest would place his hands on the head of the animal being sacrificed as a symbolic way of announcing that he, on behalf of the people of Israel, was offering his life back to God. And, later in the ceremony, the blood would be sprinkled over the assembled worshippers, a sign that the perfect sacrifice had dealt with their guilt and made them clean from the moral and spiritual contamination that separated them from God.

Those early followers of Jesus were quick to grasp that, in the death of Jesus, the symbolism of the sacrificial system had reached fulfilment. That's the reason for the many references to 'the blood' of Jesus. His death, they were convinced, was the reality to which the old rites and rituals pointed. It could not be explained simply as another Roman execution. This was what their religion had been longing for, not an animal symbolically offered on an altar, but a willing sacrifice, an act of obedience and compassion that gave them an assurance that by faith they were part of his sacrifice, that they had been made clean, that they were reconciled to God.

Powerful pictures such as ransom and sacrifice, like Isaiah's picture of the one who bears our punishment, help us not simply or even primarily to understand the

cross intellectually but to apprehend it with our imaginations and to claim its benefits by faith. The danger
when they are used as the foundation for rigid theories
is that these liberating pictures become legalistic pris-
ons. They reduce the self-giving love of Jesus to a religious system and that's exactly the opposite of what
Jesus came to do. The beauty of the cross, embracing a
world in love, is replaced by boundaries limiting who
can come and how they can make their approach.

Perspectives

There is one final direction from which we must come in
order to appreciate more fully the awesome splendour
of the death of Jesus. For those of us in the evangelical
tradition, we have normally viewed the work of Christ
on the cross solely from the perspective of personal salvation. The atoning work of Jesus is something to be
appropriated by the individual in an act of faith. Such an
approach has given rise to some of the greatest expressions of Christian devotion. A few lines from one of Isaac
Watts's hymns will serve as a perfect example

> Was it for sins that I have done
>> He suffered on the tree?
> Amazing pity, grace unknown,
>> And love beyond degree . . .
> Dear Saviour, I can ne'er repay
>> The debt of love I owe!
> Here, Lord, I give myself away:
>> Tis all that I can do.[1]

This undoubtedly represents one of the most important
strands of the saving work of Jesus on the cross. *But of*

itself it is an incomplete understanding of the death of Jesus.
Indeed, our almost exclusive emphasis on this one
aspect, to the detriment of others, has left us with a
skewed perspective and a diminished appreciation of
the work of Jesus. We need to recover something of the
broader understanding of the cross, which earlier generations held dear, and which allow us to set the image of
the man on the cross against the wider perspective of
human history, eternal spiritual realities and the entire
created order.

It is Irenaeus, Bishop of Lyon in the second century,
whose deep insight introduces us to a wider vista in seeing the truth about the cross. He drew his insight from a
sentence in the Letter to the Ephesians where Paul
writes that God will 'bring all things . . . together' in
Christ (Eph. 1:10). The Greek word which is translated
by that phrase is *anakephalaiousthai*. The prefix *ana* means
'again' and *kephale* means 'head' in English. So the word
that Paul is using can also bear the meaning of sum-
marising, going over the main points (heads) again, – in
other words, to *recapitulate*. Reflecting on this and on
New Testament passages that draw a comparison
between Adam (whose disobedience brought sin into
the world) and Christ (whose death brought salvation),
Irenaeus viewed the life and death of Jesus as a *recapitu-
lation*, a dramatic re-enactment of the entire course of
history, in which, by his perfect obedience to God culmi-
nating in his sacrificial death, Jesus reverses the effects of
our sin and renews the entire created order.

Irenaeus' dramatic and dynamic picture of the cosmic
scope of the ministry of Jesus has two enormous positive
implications as it opens us to greater vistas of beauty than
we could have imagined. In the first place, it helps us to
appreciate the magnitude of Christ's redemptive work. It
guards against a narrow individualistic understanding of

salvation: God's great purpose is not just to rescue as many souls as possible from eternal damnation; his greater and larger project is to create a new humanity in Christ and we who trust in his death and open our lives to his Spirit are the forerunners of that new humanity.

Secondly, it challenges an over-spiritual view of life. The Early Church had to resist the pressure of Greek philosophy and the popular mystery religions of the day, which had a low view of the physical realm and the material universe. In their view, only the spiritual was of real and lasting significance; the material world was the creation of an inferior god or even of some evil deity. The whole point of religious activity in this way of thinking is to escape into some spiritual realm. The Christian gospel takes a very different view. God is the Creator of the spiritual and the physical realms and he is not merely in the business of 'saving souls'. The cross culminated not in the death of Jesus, or even the survival of his spirit after death, but in the reality of the resurrection. The Risen Lord was no ghost – the narratives of his appearances when he talked and ate with his disciples make that clear. And his resurrection carries the promise that our bodies, too, will be raised and that the entire created order – a new heaven and a new earth – will be purified, renewed and remade.

The cross can never be anything other than terrible in its bloody, stark and head-on confrontation with evil. But nor can it ever be less than beautiful in its conquest of evil, not by power or force but by sheer love. It is the ultimate manifestation of reality, both divine and human, a terrible beauty that hurts us deeply to look on it and yet holds us closely by its extravagant grace and in its infinitely desirable embrace. As Rowan Williams so aptly expresses its paradoxical wonder: 'In the story of the cross and resurrection, darkness and light, terror and joy, loss and fullness are woven together in one word of grace and promise. The ray of darkness is not different from the dart of love."[2]

Three

priority: following the Master

Leaving home

John and Gertrude Haemerken must have had mixed feelings when they said goodbye to their thirteen-year-old son Thomas and watched him set off for school. This was no typical 'Monday-morning-start-of-term' departure, for Thomas was leaving his home town of Kempen in Germany for the school at Deventer in Holland to which his older brother had gone some ten years earlier. Thomas's family name of Haemerken – which means 'little hammer' – suggests that, in plying his trade as a metal worker, his father was following a profession that had been handed down through the generations. But John and Gertrude had other plans for their sons. The school at Deventer was run by the Brothers of the Common Life and Thomas's parents must have known that, like his older brother, their younger son would be destined to share the monastic life of those who would provide his education.

Thomas was an eager and apt student and did indeed become a devout and dutiful monk. His skill and diligence in copying manuscripts allowed him to contribute to the life of the order through the money raised by his work. But he also found time to compose a significant number of original writings – a chronicle of his monastery, a number of biographies and many tracts concerning the devotional life of those whose chief concern was to follow Jesus closely. Most of these are now known only to scholars and students of mediaeval monasticism. But one of his devotional works has been printed again and again across the centuries. Some would even say that, after the Bible, it has been the most influential book ever written on the Christian life. None of his fellow monks could have dreamed that their companion – this short, stooped, fresh-faced brother with the soft brown eyes who preferred his books and quiet corners to lively conversations – would be revered down through the ages. But such is the case: *The Imitation of Christ*, arguably the greatest devotional classic in all Christian literature, has ensured that his name is known by millions.

The irony is, however, that few of his readers would have any idea of his family name. Indeed, the name of Thomas Haemerken would have meant little even during his lifetime. For, after his arrival at school in Deventer, he was always referred to as 'Thomas from Kempen', the name that has come down to us as Thomas à Kempis. But somehow, that seems just right for the monk who left his native land as a boy, gave up the comfort of home, relinquished the closeness of family ties and embarked on a life of total commitment. Modest and shy he may have been by temperament, but he was fierce in his insistence that discipleship is a costly road to walk. His often quoted words on what it means to follow Christ make for uncomfortable and uncompromising reading

Jesus has always many who love His heavenly kingdom, but few who bear His cross. He has many who desire consolation, but few who care for trial. He finds many to share His table, but few to take part in His fasting. All desire to be happy with Him; few wish to suffer anything for Him. Many follow Him to the breaking of bread, but few to the drinking of the chalice of His passion. Many revere His miracles; few approach the shame of the Cross. Many love Him as long as they encounter no hardship; many praise and bless Him as long as they receive some comfort from Him . . . Those, on the contrary, who love Him for His own sake and not for any comfort of their own, bless Him in all trial and anguish of heart as well as in the bliss of consolation. Even if He should never give them consolation, yet they would continue to praise Him and wish always to give Him thanks. What power there is in pure love for Jesus – love that is free from all self-interest and self-love![3]

Of course, much of what Thomas a Kempis has to say in his writings reflects his monastic vocation and affirms an asceticism that is certainly not the calling of all Christians and that may even be questionable as a true interpretation of what it means to take up the cross and follow Jesus. But for all that, he has much to teach us. Our affluent, materialistic western culture has influenced and eroded our understanding of discipleship far more than we realise. The gospels leave us in no doubt that Jesus challenged men and women to take up their cross and follow him, to give up all selfish ambition and emulate his way of living. And yet, for much of my life, that seems to have been the aspect of the Christian message that has been neglected, or at least under-emphasised. As I reflect on the versions of the gospel I have encountered over the years, I think there have been five big emphases, all of them right in their own way, but none of them quite hitting the mark when it comes to sounding the challenge to follow, to model one's life on Jesus.

The gospel of conversion

My earliest memories of gospel preaching all focus on the importance of *conversion*, on the challenge to repent, to be born again. I heard over and over again that nothing I could do would ever make me right with God and that even my best actions were 'as filthy rags' in his sight. I was taught that only a personal experience of his forgiveness and renewal would serve to make me a truly good person, rescue me from hell and fit me for heaven. Whilst it was usually recognised that there were some people who could not pinpoint the moment of their conversion, nonetheless it was vital that such a moment should take place. I grew up in a tradition where this was not only orthodox belief; it also governed the conduct of our services and even influenced the architecture of our buildings. At the front of our halls was always the simple bench, known variously as the mercy seat, the penitents' form, or simply the place of prayer and every public act of worship would culminate in an appeal for sinners or those who wanted to know Jesus better to step forward and kneel there.

I owe so much to that tradition. I made my own first immature but totally sincere commitment to Christ as an eight-year-old boy on a 'decision Sunday', a day set aside to encourage us kids to 'ask Jesus into our hearts'. It certainly had the strength of impressing on me that the gospel demanded a response, that I needed God's forgiveness and love and that this was the most important thing I could ever do with my life. For that I will always be grateful. And yet – and it may well be my fault, I was as inattentive as most youngsters and didn't always listen as I should have done – I'm not sure that I really learned much about what it meant to follow Jesus.

The gospel of holiness

The denomination in which I grew up stands firmly in the tradition of nineteenth century holiness teaching. The Holiness Movement, as it is known, took its cue from John Wesley. After a long spiritual journey which brought him into contact with the great spiritual disciplines of catholic spirituality – prayer, fasting, meditation, intense study, self-denial – Wesley came to a realisation that, just as conversion was received by faith, so the holy life was claimed and experienced by the same means. Rather than being the reward for human effort, it was to be received by an act of faith in God. Nonetheless, Wesley continued to believe and teach that the moment at which 'entire sanctification' was received by faith was both preceded and followed by a life of spiritual discipline.

The Holiness Movement, however, placed almost all its emphasis on the insistence that holiness was a 'second blessing' distinct from conversion to be received instantaneously by faith and by every Christian who desired to live the 'higher life'. There is no doubt that for countless sincere Christians this teaching was liberating and empowering; some of the great, unsung saints of the Church are to be found in this tradition. Their simple but sincere personal piety and their integrity in matters of business often stood as a witness to the transforming power of the gospel. But it did have some inherent weaknesses. Two in particular have been noticeable.

Firstly, the stress on holiness as *an experience to be claimed by faith* led almost inevitably to a sense that it was *an experience which had to be preserved*. This, in turn, led to an undue concentration on inner, spiritual feelings rather than to an emphasis on ongoing spiritual growth. And secondly, it had a tendency to degenerate over the years into an understanding of sanctity which was little more than a kind of narrow legalism in which the holy life was expressed primarily in abstinence from 'worldly pleasures' such as dancing, the cinema, alcohol and tobacco. Concentrating on New Testament passages from the Epistles – which could be cited as proof texts for its theology of 'a second blessing' – rather than on the life and teaching of Jesus, it often had little to say about what it really means to be a follower of Jesus.

The gospel of truth

As I grew older and began to discover something of the life of the wider Church beyond my own denomination, I encountered the solid teaching of the reformed tradition, with its emphasis on biblical truth and its concentration on the clear and plain exposition of Scripture. It was something I needed to hear and it continues to influence my life to this day. Indeed, I guess that many of my friends and colleagues, if asked, would describe me as primarily an expository preacher. I'd be proud to have that designation on my tombstone! In a world of relativism where truth is often whatever you want it to be and where clear standards of conduct have been lost, there is a definite need for an unequivocal declaration of gospel certainties.

But again, I have found it an insufficient and incomplete gospel. At its best, it draws us to the written word of God to seek his heart and discern his will. But this, too, has limitations. There is a temptation to 'bibliolatry', to place the written word above the living word – Jesus himself; there is a danger of reducing the challenge of the gospel to nothing more than an intellectual apprehension of biblical truths and an assent to doctrinal propositions; there is sometimes an element of hard and legalistic pharisaism in which the gospel is reduced to isolated texts which become rigid rules; and it has all too often produced church members who are sermon-tasters and devotees of good preaching rather than passionate and radical followers of Jesus.

The gospel of baptism in the Spirit

The wave of charismatic renewal which swept across Britain in the 1970s did much to reinvigorate the Church. To borrow a phrase, we no longer just 'talked about the stuff' in the gospel stories, we began to see it in action. The Holy Spirit, who for so long had been the neglected member of the Trinity, was suddenly present among us. The God of the Bible was not merely a distant historical truth; he was a living, life-transforming reality. The way we approached worship changed; instead of singing hymns *about* God, we began to address our praises *to* him. It changed the way we understood spiritual warfare; instead of being a pious metaphor, the great battle between good and evil became a powerful meeting of spiritual forces; and it changed the way in which we viewed our membership of the Body of Christ; instead of being content to be pew-fillers, we became participants, gifted and equipped by the Spirit of God.

It seemed things were set fair for a new dawn and prophecies abounded assuring us that revival was just around the corner. Alas, the mighty army of the living God succumbed all too easily to the temptation to become a holy huddle, sharing our words of knowledge, getting 'blessed out of our socks', rushing from one charismatic conference to the next, neglecting the disciplines of study and meditation and assuming that the infilling of the Holy Spirit provided us with a short-cut to spiritual maturity. As if that was not enough, we allowed ourselves to be diverted from our calling to discipleship into a detour in which our primary pre-occupation was debating whether the baptism in the Spirit was a second blessing or not and whether speaking in tongues was the necessary evidence that it had taken place. Despite much that was positive, we made all too little progress in becoming true followers of Jesus.

The gospel of grace

Few books, if any, in recent years have made such an impact on Christians on both sides of the Atlantic as Philip Yancey's *What's so amazing about grace?*[4] One reviewer described it as 'beyond doubt the best book I have read from a Christian author in my life' and there is no disputing that Yancey has done the whole Church a great service in addressing the subject of grace. He calls it 'our last best word' and insists that it 'contains the essence of the gospel as a drop of water can contain the image of the sun'. In the course of almost three hundred pages, he reminds us that grace is the heart of the gospel message; that there is nothing bad we can do that will make God love us any the less and nothing good we can do that will make God love us any the more; that the task of the Church is to dispense grace generously and extravagantly to all kinds and conditions of people; and that we must never constrain grace within our theological systems or our denominational structures. Yancey has done us a great service in drawing us back to the gospel of grace.

But – and here I tread warily, such is my respect for Yancey's presentation and my sense that he is right in insisting that grace is the very essence of the gospel – I would dare to suggest that there is something more to be said. That something more is this: *grace is unconditional, but it is also uncompromising and unsettling*. It is beyond dispute that grace means that God accepts us just as we are and that his acceptance and forgiveness are given freely. But grace also means that God will not stop until he has made us all that he wants us to be. *A gracious God wants to transform needy sinners into Christlike saints; he wants us to be part not merely of a believing community but of a new humanity*. And that work of transformation will always be painstaking on his part and often painful on ours. Receiving grace is far from being the passport to a peaceful life. It is much more like registering for a marathon race. There's a long journey ahead and there will be many miles to cover, many steps to be taken, before the race is complete. And the training will sometimes hurt to the point where you'll be tempted to wish you had been content to remain a couch potato.

The call to follow

When God dispenses grace, people always find themselves on the move! And it will be as real and as life-changing as Thomas à Kempis's journey from Kempen to Deventer. For Noah, it meant building an ark; for

Abraham, it meant uprooting from his family home and heading for a future and a land about which he knew nothing; for Moses, it meant walking straight back into Egypt and into danger; for Nehemiah, it meant leaving the security of the court, returning to a ruined city and supervising a building project that upset many of his neighbours; for Amos, it meant leaving the pastoral simplicity of his flock and his fig trees and embarking on a costly prophetic ministry to a reluctant audience; for the first disciples, it meant walking away from the family fishing business and following Jesus to Jerusalem and Calvary; for Saul, from Tarsus it meant taking an entirely different stance on everything he had previously believed and held dear. And for all of them, it meant that things would never be the same and that life would never be easy again.

Throughout the gospels, the offer of grace is always bound up with an invitation to get up and follow the One who makes the offer. The public ministry of Jesus begins with a joyful declaration to an occupied people that the Kingdom of God has broken through; but the declaration is followed by a demand for repentance – an about turn, a change of mind and a change of direction (Mk. 1:14,15). To be part of his inner circle was a rare privilege; in the religious culture of the day prospective disciples had to apply to a rabbi who would accept them only if he thought they were good enough. Jesus is different: he *chooses* his disciples and they are working class men, not élite students; but he lets them know that he is about to turn their lives upside down – they'll be after bigger fish from here on in (Mk. 1:16;17). And when he addresses the crowd of interested listeners who follow him for his stories and his miracles, he leaves them in no doubt as to just what it will mean to respond to his gracious summons:

> If anyone would come after me, he must deny himself
> and take up his cross and follow me. For whoever wants
> to save his life will lose it, but whoever loses his life for
> me and the gospel will save it (Mk. 8:34,35).

The offer of grace is inextricably bound up with an invitation to attend your own funeral. The paradox of the gospel is that the way to self-fulfilment is to abandon all thought of self and surrender totally to a life of following Jesus.

The inescapable conclusion is this: the priority of the gospel is a call to follow and all those other aspects of gospel truth take their place only as we follow; *conversion* happens *in the following of Jesus; holiness* grows *in the following; truth* is understood in *the following; the Holy Spirit* drenches and empowers us *in the following; grace* is experienced *in the following*. What that means in practice is no different for us from what it was for the first disciples – 'that they might be with him and that he might send them out to preach and have authority to drive out demons' (Mk. 3:14,15). We, too, are called to share the life and the ministry of Jesus, expressing through our lives and in our day the terrible beauty that is always manifest when evil is confronted, when the sins and hurts of our fellow human beings are embraced and when hopeless situations are redeemed and transformed by self-giving love. Just as Jesus led the Twelve through the towns and villages of Galilee – attending weddings and funerals, preaching in synagogues, eating with the marginalized, bringing healing to the sick and the dying, replacing the tepid water of religion with the sparkling wine of new life – so he calls us to express our discipleship in the everyday things of life, transforming them with the terrible beauty of grace.

Thinking hard

If it is true that the priority of the gospel is to follow Jesus, then there is some hard thinking to be done by those of us who claim to be his followers. Three questions in particular demand serious consideration.

What's the main thing?

It's something of a cliché, but it bears repeating, nonetheless: the main thing is always to keep the main thing the main thing. And the main thing for the Church is to follow the Master, to live as he lived, to be his body on earth. What characterised his ministry was his openness to God and his self-less love for others. Every individual Christian, every local church, every denomination, every church stream and every ministry must constantly ask if the main thing really is the main thing. Like any other group of human beings, churches can degenerate into hotbeds of personal power struggles and battle-grounds for competing parties. Or they can focus on their own survival rather than being willing to live and die for others. Perhaps the greatest temptation of all in these days is to wallow in nostalgia and to long for the return of Christendom, for a fast fading age in which the Church enjoyed a privileged, powerful and protected position. As Tony Campolo once courageously said at a denominational conference at which he was the guest speaker, 'If the 1950s ever come back, you're ready for it!' Alas, those days will never return. But that very fact may help us to remember our true calling – to follow the Master, to die to privilege and power and to be what we are called to be. Stuart Murray presents the options and the opportunities that face us as we rediscover our calling:

The near future will be difficult for Christians in a society that has rejected institutional Christianity and is
familiar enough with the Christian story not to want to
hear it again . . . But perhaps – if we have the courage to
face into this future rather than hankering after a fading
past, if we resist short-term strategies and pre-packaged
answers, if we learn to be cross-cultural missionaries in
our own society and if we can negotiate the next forty
years – whatever culture emerges from the ruins of
Christendom might offer tremendous opportunities for
telling and living out the Christian story in a society
where this is largely unknown . . . Christendom is dying,
but a new and dynamic Christianity could arise from its
ashes.[5]

What's our message?

If that really is the main thing for us, then the inescapable
conclusion is that the message of the Church, above
everything else, should be a call to follow Jesus.
Everything thing we do and say and, above all, everything we are, should constitute a demonstration of love
and grace that will draw people to Jesus to experience
those things for themselves and then to give their lives to
the great purpose of following him. Sadly, there are millions living around us who have been left with the
impression that the main thing for the Christian Church
is to find out how and where people are enjoying themselves and to put a stop to it! Of course, we are right to be
concerned about the shallowness of our materialistic,
self-centred entertainment culture. And certainly we
need to raise our voices in protest against the erosion of
moral standards that threaten the fabric of marriage and
family life. But somehow we often do so in a way that
lacks the sympathy and empathy that Jesus always

demonstrated to people who were guilty of sin. We tell ourselves that we are speaking prophetically, but to our hearers it just sounds as if we're angry and unpleasant people.

Some time ago, to the surprise of my friends, I made a guest appearance on the *Jeremy Kyle show*! (If you're not familiar with this particular television programme, I can best describe it as the UK's answer to Jerry Springer – an opportunity for sad and troubled people to 'wash their dirty linen in public'.) This particular edition of the show, however, was a little different. It involved a live-link to a church in the USA whose members are notorious for two things: at the funerals of American service personnel killed in action, they parade with placards declaring that the deaths of these young people represent the judgement of an angry God; and they take a virulently anti-gay stance.

I had been asked to be the third member of a panel with a woman whose son had been killed on active service in Iraq and the publicity officer for the Gay and Lesbian Federation in the north west of England. The three members of the church on the screen in front of us (all wearing T-shirts with the slogan 'God Hates Fags'!) proceeded to tell the bereaved mother that her son was in hell and that his death was part of God's wrathful judgement on our nation. Their words to the young gay man sitting beside me were so unpleasant that I wouldn't even repeat them. And their message to the television audience was spelt out bluntly: 'God hates you until you repent!'

I felt deeply ashamed of these 'fellow-Christians'. I know that their position is so unpleasant and extreme that it represents only a tiny vocal minority of misguided Christians. But what troubled me even more than their hate-filled words was the realisation that my colleagues on the panel and many of the studio audience were under the impression that this was typical of the attitude of Christians to those whom they have designated as sinners. How very different we have become from Jesus, who was constantly in hot water with religious people for the way in which he fraternised with sinners, sought them out, ate with them, befriended them and left them in no doubt that God loved them whatever wrong they might have done. It was that very love and acceptance that set them free to move on in grace and begin to become the kind of people God wanted them to be. It is time for us to create the kind of loving communities that accept and embrace every kind of sinner, the kind of churches where the more fellow-disciples know about us and about our weaknesses and failings, the more they love us. That's when people really hear the call of Jesus clearly.

Where's the Master?

Most of the time when my daughters were children, they got along together like good sisters should. But, from time to time, disputes would break out between them that could only be resolved by an appeal to my fatherly wisdom. Usually that meant sending them to different parts of the house until their tempers had cooled. On one occasion the reason for their quarrel was a book of Bible stories, of all things! I'm not really sure that it was an indication of their childhood piety, but both of them asserted ownership and both of them insisted on reading the book at the same time. They decided to resolve matters by trying to tug the book out of each other's hands. It took only a few minutes of this unpromising method of resolution for the book to be ripped apart. Jeni was left holding the covers while Catriona had the rest of the book. It was at this point they decided that, once again, I would have to adjudicate. So Catriona came to me with tears streaming down her face saying, 'Look, Daddy, Jesus has come out of the book.'

Like all preachers I've been grateful for the sermon illustrations with which my kids have provided me and I've used that one more than a few times over the years. And here's the point of telling it now. It's time for us to wake up to the fact that we cannot keep Jesus inside a book, inside a denominational structure, inside a particular culture or theological system. Just as he does in the gospel stories, he turns up in unlikely places and unlikely people. Dare I suggest that sometimes when we're engaged in our church activities, Jesus is somewhere else – and he's calling people to follow him.

Let me offer one example of what I mean. I have a number of friends who are alcoholics and who have benefited tremendously from the twelve step programme of Alcoholics Anonymous. Recently, I sat down with them and read through those twelve steps. The ruthless honesty of these words, their openness to God and their very deliberate marking out of the path to recovery make these sentences both moving and challenging.

We

1. Admitted we were powerless over alcohol – that our lives had become unmanageable.
2. Came to believe that a Power greater than ourselves could restore us to sanity.
3. Made a decision to turn our will and our lives over to the care of God *as we understood Him*.
4. Made a searching and fearless moral inventory of ourselves.
5. Admitted to God, to ourselves and to another human being the exact nature of our wrongs.

6. Were entirely ready to have God remove all these defects of character.
7. Humbly asked Him to remove our shortcomings.
8. Made a list of all persons we had harmed and became willing to make amends to them all.
9. Made direct amends to such people wherever possible, except when to do so would injure them or others.
10. Continued to take personal inventory and when we were wrong promptly admitted it.
11. Sought through prayer and meditation to improve our conscious contact with God, *as we understood Him*, praying only for knowledge of His will for us and the power to carry that out.
12. Having had a spiritual awakening as the result of these steps, we tried to carry this message to alcoholics and to practice these principles in all our affairs.

As I read those words and discussed them with my friends, I couldn't escape the conviction that this is nothing other than a discipleship course, that in undergoing this programme, people are in some sense really meeting Jesus and hearing his call to follow. They are opening their lives to grace, not only in its acceptance but also in its ongoing and costly challenge to change. Of course, I understand – and share – the objection that we Christians make instinctively: those phrases about 'God as we understood him' fall short of the truth that has been revealed to us in Scripture. But then I remember the story in John's gospel of the man who was cured of his blindness by Jesus. The religious leaders insisted to him that the healing could not have come from Jesus; in their book he was a sinner. The man's reply is deeply uncomfortable to those who insist on sound doctrine as a pre-condition to receiving grace and healing: 'Whether he is a sinner or not, I don't know. One thing I do know. I was blind but now I see' (Jn. 9:25).

Those words force me to face the truth of which I am becoming increasingly aware. It is not necessary to have a perfect theology, or even a full understanding of who Jesus is, to receive his grace and to follow him. In fact none of us has a perfect intellectual or theological grasp of those truths. It's enough that we are willing to follow. The truth can be – must be – worked out from that starting point.

My thinking was challenged even further when my friends shared with me the fact that in all their time of attending AA meetings, they had met only one other person who claimed to be a Christian. And that one other person had said to them, 'I've found in AA what I never managed to find in the church.' I am forced to ask uncomfortable questions. Could it be that Jesus is sometimes more fully present in places like AA, where people realise their desperate need of each other and of God's help, than in many a church meeting where we are tempted to trust in our own abilities and in the trappings of worship and church life? Could it be that, rather than we Christians 'taking Jesus' into the world, we actually need to find out where he is and what he is doing and, by our humble testimony and our authentic Christian living, help people to understand the One who stands in their midst? And could it be that the words of Albert Schweitzer have more truth and more relevance to us than we who stand in the evangelical tradition have often been willing to recognize?

> He comes to us as One unknown, without a name, as of old, by the lake side, He came to those men who knew Him not. He speaks to us the same word: "Follow thou

me!" and sets us to the tasks which He has to fulfil for
our time. He commands. And to those who obey Him,
whether they be wise or simple, He will reveal Himself
in the toils, the conflicts, the sufferings which they shall
pass through in His fellowship and, as an ineffable mystery, they shall learn in their own experience Who He is.[6]

Four

progress: becoming like Jesus

Wearing their hearts on their sleeves

For the eleven footballers chosen to wear the colours of Heart of Midlothian, match-day on the 11 November 2007 was very different from their usual experience. In the morning, the entire team, known to their fans simply as 'Hearts', attended the Remembrance Day service at Edinburgh's Haymarket. Then, in the afternoon, they took the field for their Scottish Premier League game against Aberdeen, wearing a brand new strip in the club's traditional maroon colours. However, this was not part of the usual marketing tactics employed by most football clubs to encourage parents to spend yet more money on replica shirts for their kids in the run-up to Christmas. This kit would be worn only once, for this was Armistice Sunday and embroidered on the sleeve were the names of seven young men – seven young men who will never be forgotten in Edinburgh: John Allan, James Boyd, Duncan Currie, Ernest Ellis, Thomas Gracie, James Speedie and Harry Wattie. At the end of the match, the shirts were washed, framed and auctioned for charity.

The story behind this unusual tribute is one that is told often whenever football people gather together in Scotland's capital city. In 1914, Hearts had won their first eight games of the season and were sitting proudly on top of the Scottish First Division. Newspaper reports of the day make it very clear that all of their fans and most of the pundits back then believed that they were the finest eleven ever to wear the maroon jerseys. The people of Edinburgh were in no doubt that, by the end of the season, their team would fulfil their destiny as league champions. But they reckoned without the intervention of a Serbian terrorist in a far-off land about which most Edinburgh folk certainly knew very little and probably cared even less. But when Gavrilo Princip fired the shot that killed the Archduke Franz Ferdinand, the heir to the Austro-Hungarian throne, on the steps of the Sarajevo Town Hall in June 1914, he set off a train of events that would deprive the Hearts team and their supporters of their well-deserved and long-anticipated triumph. Within months of that assassination, World War One had broken out and the prospect of a national football victory seemed of little consequence when compared to an armed conflict of global proportions.

And that's why, in November 1914, the entire Hearts team marched to the army recruiting office in Edinburgh, becoming the only football club in Britain whose entire team enlisted for action. Within a few short weeks they were no longer footballers; instead, they were fighting men, part of the 16th Royal Scots and the uniform of the British Army had replaced the maroon of their beloved football club. If they had ever imagined that running around a football pitch on a wintry Saturday afternoon in Scotland was tough, they were to be disabused of such naivety all too soon. The 16th Royal Scots were in the thick of the terrible and bloody Battle of the Somme which lasted from 1 July to 18 November 1916. The death toll was tragically high. Almost sixty thousand British troops were killed at the Somme, one third of them on the first day of the battle. And among those who lost their lives were the seven members of the Hearts team whose names were remembered and whose sacrifice was honoured more than ninety years later.

To accuse the footballers who carried the names of the fallen on their sleeves of nostalgia or sentimentality would be absurd and offensive. Who could fail to be moved by the extravagant gesture of patriotism and the passionate commitment to King and country of the 'magnificent seven'? Even those of us who espouse non-violence as integral to our understanding of the gospel and who see all war as a terrible expression of evil, recognise the noble self-sacrifice of those who are willing to fight and die for freedom and the terrible beauty of lives given for a greater good and the sake of others. An act of solemn remembrance is the very least that we can do. In truth, such moments are more than just an expression of respect for past sacrifices; they are points of reference on the journey of life, causing us to affirm what is good and of lasting value and encouraging us to live in a manner that is worthy of the price they paid.

Sharing the hospitality of the Lord's table

Followers of Jesus should, of course, be the first to acknowledge the validity of such acts of remembrance and their importance to the spiritual health of any community. For two thousand years, we have renewed and refreshed our commitment to follow Jesus by remembering and re-enacting his words and deeds at his final meal with the disciples as he prepared them for his death.

Whenever we share in the Lord's Supper we are acknowledging the truth that we make progress in following Jesus only by deliberately and constantly re-focussing on and re-aligning our lives with the terrible beauty of his sacrificial death. The failure to make that journey humbly, spiritually, emotionally and imaginatively will have terrible consequences.

Life in first century Corinth, with its slave-based economy, its prevailing Greek culture and its pagan temples, was in many ways very different from life in twenty-first century Britain. But Paul's letter to the young church in that city reveals a group of people much closer to us than we might at first imagine. Like us, they wrestled with issues related to what they should believe, how they should behave and how they should relate to each other and the world around them. And in two crucial areas of life, Paul challenges them – and us – to a true understanding of what the ceremony and symbolism of the Lord's Supper really means for followers of Jesus.

Participation

It was the predominance of pagan religion in Corinth that gave rise to the first problem. There were more than a dozen temples in the city dedicated to the worship of various gods; but the best known was that of Aphrodite, the goddess of love and sex, whose one thousand priestesses would descend on the city as darkness fell and ply their trade as prostitutes. Corinth was in such thrall to the cult that it was difficult to live there and remain untouched by it in some way. It's unlikely that those early converts to Christianity indulged in the grosser expressions of this pagan religion, but we know from Paul's letters to the Corinthian church that their lives were touched by it in at least one way. Apparently there was some confusion as to whether they should share in meals, in which food that had been offered to idols was subsequently served at table. Some felt that their new-found freedom in Christ – with its assurance that gods of pagan religion were no gods at all – allowed them to share in these occasions. Others were not so sure.

Characteristically, Paul does not simply moralise on the issue; instead, he takes the opportunity to highlight a crucial aspect of authentic Christian experience which he relates to their *participation* in the Lord's Supper. In fact, that is precisely the issue – their participation in something more than mere ritual. Just as the footballers and spectators in Edinburgh recognised that their common humanity linked them with those seven young men who gave their lives in war, so – and at an infinitely deeper level – those who share in the act of communion are acknowledging that their lives are bound up with Jesus and involved in his sacrificial death. To appreciate that is to understand that any contact with idol worship or occult practices is ludicrous and obscene

> Therefore, my dear friends, flee from idolatry. I speak to sensible people; judge for yourselves what I say. Is not the cup of thanksgiving for which we give thanks a participation in the blood of Christ? And is not the bread that we break a participation in the body of Christ? Because there is one loaf, we, who are many, are one body, for we all partake of the one loaf (1 Cor. 10:14–17).

It is worth noting that the word in the original Greek, which is rendered as 'participation' in the passage above, is *koinonia*, a word which elsewhere in the New Testament is often translated as 'fellowship'. Paul's thinking is not difficult to follow. When we share in the

Lord's Supper, when together in faith we repeat Jesus' words and actions, we are dramatically expressing and reinforcing a great truth. We are part of a new community, a community of believers, who not only *benefit* from the sacrifice made at Calvary, but whose whole identity is derived from the fact that spiritually we *share* in that act of sacrifice. In sharing the cup and the loaf, we are acknowledging and declaring that we have indeed *become* the Body of Christ and that the terrible beauty of his brokenness – his life lived for others, his infinite forgiveness, his atoning death, his passion for the lost, the last and the least – all of these must be seen in us. And consequently, the pleasures we enjoy and the practices we shun, the places we happily go to and the places we avoid, the causes we embrace and the issues against which we stand – all of these are decided not primarily by a rigid code of ethics but by a rigorous commitment to Jesus. We make progress as disciples not by observing a strict morality but by pursuing a deeper intimacy with Jesus and by a clearer expression of our identity as his Body on earth.

Proclamation

The second issue that Paul addresses arises from the blatant denial of these very realities in the practice of the Lord's Supper in the Corinthian church. It should have been a moving reflection on and strengthening reinforcement of their identity, as humble participants in Jesus' sacrificial offering; it should have been a powerful reminder of their unity as his Body in the world. In fact, it was anything but those things. Tragically and ironically, the fellowship meal, of which the Lord's Supper formed the climax, had degenerated into a frenzy of rivalry and an orgy of gluttony and drunkenness. Paul does not mince his words in addressing the problem

> When you come together, it is not the Lord's Supper you eat, for as you eat, each of you goes ahead without waiting for anybody else. One remains hungry, another gets drunk. Don't you have homes to eat and drink in? Or do you despise the church of God and humiliate those who have nothing? What shall I say to you? Shall I praise you for this? Certainly not! (1 Cor. 11:20–22)

But, as before, the apostle is not content simply to moralise; once again he takes them deep into the meaning of the ceremony of the cup and the loaf and, in effect, to the heart of what it means to follow Jesus

> For I received from the Lord what I also passed on to you: The Lord Jesus, on the night he was betrayed, took bread, and when he had given thanks, he broke it and said, "This is my body, which is for you; do this in remembrance of me." In the same way, after supper he took the cup, saying, "This cup is the new covenant in my blood; do this, whenever you drink it, in remembrance of me." *For whenever you eat this bread and drink this cup, you proclaim the Lord's death until he comes* (my italics) (1 Cor. 11:23–26).

Compressed into that final short sentence is the very essence not simply of the Lord's Supper but of authentic Christian living – *proclaiming the Lord's death until he comes*. We must share the bread and the wine with such a spirit of humility and unity that it becomes a dramatic declaration of his sacrificial life and death; and we must live in such a way that our very lives – corporately and individually – are an expression of that same self-giving love. The sacrament of the bread and wine must be reflected in the sacrament of the surrendered life which is, in itself, a proclamation of the Lord's death. Albert Orsborn's communion hymn expresses it succinctly

> My life must be Christ's broken bread,
>> My love his outpoured wine,
> A cup o'erfilled, a table spread
>> Beneath his name and sign,
> That other souls, refreshed and fed,
>> May share his life through mine.

Participating and proclaiming, refocusing on his passion and re-aligning our lives with his, sharing in the life of Jesus and showing it to the world in our own lives – those are the essential preconditions of progress in Christian living.

Living in the hope the Lord's coming

When we heed the challenge of Paul's words, we are fulfilling the task of making what happened in the past – the death of Jesus on the cross – a reality in the present tense of our lives. But there is also a future dynamic; we are to proclaim the Lord's death *'until he comes'*. The Lord's Supper – and, if what we have said above is correct, the entire witness of the Church and the whole life of every individual Christian – has an anticipatory and an eschatological dimension. By its very nature, every true expression of the gospel looks forward to a glorious consummation. For the crucified Saviour is also the risen and ascended Lord, whose coming and ultimate victory are promised throughout the New Testament. All our worship and witness must embody, at one and the same time, the passion of the cross and the promise of the completion of God's purposes in the coming of Jesus. Our faith and conduct, which are rooted in the historic events of Calvary, must be of such a character and quality that they also raise in those who witness them the hope of the kingdom of God breaking through in all its fullness. To put it another way, our lives must be the demonstration of God's love in the present that gives a watching world reason to believe that goodness and love will indeed triumph over evil and hate.

There is no more moving expression in the New Testament of how those two aspects are bound up together than that in John's first letter. It was probably written somewhere between AD 85 and 95, a time when most of the original eye-witnesses to the life and death of Jesus had themselves died and when, consequently, the hope of the gospel was beginning to dim in the eyes of some.

> How great is the love the Father has lavished on us, that we should be called children of God! And that is what we are! The reason the world does not know us is that it did not know him. Dear friends, now we are children of God, and what we will be has not yet been made known. But we know that when he appears, we shall be like him, for we shall see him as he is. Everyone who has this hope in him purifies himself, just as he is pure (1 Jn. 3:1–3).

To be *called* 'children of God' – even more, to actually *be* his children – is surely nothing more or less than to manifest our family likeness to the Father and to his Son, Jesus. It is to live in love, to live for others, to forgive the wrong that is done to us, to transform, by our Christlike living, situations where evil seems to rule into places where God reigns in love. As John bluntly reminds us, we will not always win the recognition and the plaudits of others; what was true for Jesus will also be true for us. No matter, we are children of God and we are in the process of becoming, growing ever more into his like-ness, progressing to a future that we cannot even imag-ine. But – and here is the glory and the mystery of grace, the climax of the gospel story – when Jesus Christ appears and when we seem him as he truly is, we shall be like him!

It is probably true to say that no other aspect of the gospel has attracted the kind of attention that has been given to the subject of the second coming of Jesus and 'last things'. It has been used by many an evangelist to draw fearful pictures of the end-times, designed to scare unwilling and inattentive sinners into a shocked realisa-tion of their eternal destiny. If that worked in the past, it certainly doesn't seem to be very effective today. It has been used by those who have imagined that the Book of Revelation resembles nothing so much as a railway timetable; they have applied their interpretations of selected passages to work out the details of the end of the world; they have debated pre-millennialism, post-millennialism and a-millennialism; and they have come up with conflicting dates and times which have subse-quently been proved to be no more than the work of their imagination. It has been used as the basis for an entire series of novels which for some have been block-busting best-sellers, and for others have seemed to be of little literary merit and of even less theological value.

Somehow, all of these seem a long way from the pre-vailing tenor of the passages in the New Testament that speak of Christ's coming. They neither satisfy our curiosity for dates and details, nor provide us with material to frighten sinners into the love of God. Rather they insist on the ultimate victory of Christ and on the security of those who trust in him, whatever may be happening in the world around them. And here in these few verses from John's letter they hold out the promise that, when he appears, we shall be like him, for we shall see him as he really is. The obvious question is: what does it mean when it says that we will be *like* Jesus? It surely does not infer a physical resemblance and it certainly cannot mean that we become 'the same as' the divine Son of God. I want to suggest that the answer lies in those resurrection appearances where the suffering humanity of the Risen Christ is revealed in the wounds in his hands and side. Sometimes - too often – the coming Christ is pictured as a mighty warrior carrying all before him. Too easily we forget the truth that Matthew Bridges expresses in his great triumphal hymn of the coming kingdom – that the risen and ascended Lord is the Christ of the cross

> Crown him the Lord of love:
>   Behold his hands and side,
> Those wounds yet visible above,
>   In beauty glorified;
> All hail, Redeemer, hail!
>   For thou hast died for me;
> Thy praise and glory shall not fail
>   Throughout eternity.

Those 'wounds yet visible above' are the hallmarks of the terrible beauty of God's perfect sacrifice, a life given for others, a searing love that remains in the heart of God for all eternity. To 'see him as he is' will be to come face to face with the enormity of his love, to be willingly and joyfully overwhelmed by it, to be completely transformed by it and to share it for all eternity.

That's why John does not follow those words by inviting us to pause and wonder at the love the Father has lavished on us, far less to speculate on the details of how and when God will bring his work to completion. Instead, he immediately issues us with a challenge: 'since we have this hope, we must purify ourselves just as he is pure.' Commentators and preachers will often point out that this is a call to holy living; and they are not wrong to do so. Usually we understand such holiness in terms of moral purity – integrity in business, fidelity in marriage, responsibility to church and state. Again, this is certainly not wrong. But I suspect that it is far less than what John is saying.

The holiness of Jesus was in stark contrast to that of the Pharisees and the teachers of the law. They were upstanding members of the community, fine examples of moral rectitude. But their understanding of holiness was one that required them to abstain from contact with sinners who might contaminate them by their sinfulness. Their moral purity separated them from the impure and the undeserving. Jesus, on the other hand, believed in, taught to others and lived out a holiness which was infectious; the kind of holiness that ate with sinners, that sought out the company of the marginalized and that ultimately took him to the cross, the sign of ultimate shame for a religious Jew of the day.

To purify ourselves 'just as he is pure' means much more than observing the rules of moral righteousness. It means being touched by and being open to the terrible beauty of the cross so that we, too, begin to live in a way that bears the pain of others; it means that we, too, begin to live in a way that makes us agents of transformation, so that places of injustice and suffering become scenarios of redemption and love; it means that something of the grace of Jesus is seen in us and in every life that we touch.

Coming with healing to the world's pain

There is a snatch of song that has lodged itself in my mind since I heard it some years ago. It's a line about a love, so big and so broken by pain and suffering, that there is no limit to where it can reach, no situation so hopeless that it cannot touch and transform it. I may not be recalling the words accurately and, even if I am, it doesn't make sense logically. But it has stayed with me because, whether the song-writer intended it or not, it certainly does make sense *theologically*.

The cross is surely the ultimate example of a big and broken love that reaches us from the far side of pain and suffering, the final, indisputable proof that there is no place to which we can fall where we cannot be reached and rescued by the love of God. When we say of Jesus that he 'came back from the dead', we are guilty of lazy and inaccurate speech. Lazarus came back from the dead, was restored to life, had to do his dying all over again. But Jesus *went through* death, plumbed its depths and came out at the other side. The gospel is not about survival but about resurrection; it is the reason to believe that for every individual and every situation locked in hopelessness and frustration there is a hope and a future. If Jesus really did die on the cross and if he really was raised from the dead, then everything is changed. He really is the One who greets us from far side of pain and suffering.

And in the unknown future that awaits us, we who hope in him must live out our promise to be the followers of the crucified Christ, the bearers of the cross, and the companions of his risen presence. The true progress of the church and its people can be measured not by our numerical strength, not by our ability to influence political decisions, not by our power to bring about a

Christian culture, but by our increasing capacity to heal the hurts of the world as we love in the face of hate, forgive in the face of hurt, give in the face of greed, and serve in the face of selfishness. There is no other way in which we can come with healing to a hurting world. In the dreary day of hopelessness and the dark night of injustice in which too many of our fellow creatures live, we need to keep our promise to be bearers of the cross and people of the resurrection.

Five

power: changing the paradigm

A different kind of song

In 1866, just three years after President Abraham Lincoln had issued the Emancipation Proclamation declaring freedom for all of America's black slaves, the members of the American Missionary Association founded the Fisk School in an abandoned Union Army barracks, to provide an elementary education programme for newly liberated slaves. It was a noble act and one which history has subsequently vindicated; the Fisk University is now one of America's most highly respected centres of learning. None of the teachers or scholars in those early years, however, could have imagined the glorious future of their school, for as early as 1871 the survival of the entire venture was in doubt. The coffers were empty, students were living and working in conditions that were worse than inadequate and there was a desperate need for funds.

But George Leonard White, the school's treasurer, refused to let the dream die and he hit upon a simple plan. He would take a group of the school's most gifted singers on a fund-raising tour of the northern states.

Alas, not everyone shared his enthusiasm for the project. His fellow staff members opposed the whole idea, parents were afraid to let their children travel such distances and the American Missionary Association refused to help, afraid that the choir's efforts would jeopardise their own fund-raising plans. White refused to give up: 'I'm depending on God,' he told them, 'not on you.' Using his own money, as much as he could borrow from others and the last $40 from the school's capital, he set off on 6 October 1871, with his choir to 'sing the money out of the hearts and pockets' of any audience they could muster for their concerts.

White was concerned that genteel and sophisticated white folks might not take the musical offerings of his black protégés seriously, so he tried to 'Europeanise' them as much as he could and taught them to sing light classical works and 'proper hymns' that he thought might appeal to potential audiences. The first month or so was hardly encouraging, attendances at their concerts were sparse and money came in slowly. But everything changed on the evening of 16 November when they sang from the balcony of a Congregational church in Oberlin, Ohio, to entertain a group of clergy who had gathered in conference.

The assembled ministers paid little attention until George White decided to change the repertoire and include one of the 'spirituals' that were sung often among black worshippers, but which few white congregations had heard until that point. When they began to sing 'Steal Away to Jesus' the atmosphere changed in a moment: the audience listened to the song with rapt attention, the noise of conversation was replaced by the sound of tears and the reception at the end of the song was enthusiastic beyond anything that had previously greeted the Fisk Singers. In the years ahead, their fame would spread across the world, their list of celebrity listeners would include President Ulysses S. Grant at the White House and Queen Victoria in London and they would raise the equivalent of millions of dollars for the school. And in all those places and to all those people, they sang the songs that were so much part of their unique identity and their spiritual journey.

It was not that they suddenly became better singers that evening in Oberlin. What changed was simply that they began singing a different song, a song that took them deep into who they really were and where they had come from, a song that expressed the hurt and injustice of slavery, the longing for freedom and the discovery of God in the midst of pain and suffering. When they reached back into their history and drew from their musical heritage, they unleashed a quality and an authenticity that could never be present in their renditions of light opera and popular classics. The spirituals took both singers and audiences beyond an evening of entertainment to an experience of a place where the ugliness and inhumanity of racism and economic exploitation are transformed into something beautiful by the grace of God in the human spirit.

A different kind of power

The Fisk Singers were not by any means the only or the last group of men and women to learn that we achieve little when we try to play by someone else's rules and that we are truly effective only when we are loyal to ourselves and to our heritage, when we go back to the vulnerability and weakness of our roots. To do otherwise is to court disaster. In his deeply disturbing book, *With God on Our Side: the rise of the Religious Right in America*,

William Martin quotes Chuck Colson, one of Richard
Nixon's most cynical aides in the 1970s, who later
reflected on how easily Christian leaders of the so-called
'Silent Majority' could be seduced by political power

> Nixon was a very shrewd politician. He knew how to
> use religious people to maximum advantage. He recog-
> nised that there were voting blocs that were enormously
> influenced by their religious leaders . . . We got Cardinal
> Krol in from Philadelphia and took him out on the
> *Sequoia* (the presidential yacht) and the Cardinal was just
> absolutely mesmerised by Nixon . . . At the same time,
> Nixon recognised that the evangelical vote was the key
> to the Southern strategy, so he began to invite evangeli-
> cal leaders in. And one of my jobs in the White House
> was to romance religious leaders. We would bring
> (them) into the White House and they would be dazzled
> by the aura of the Oval Office and I found them to be
> about the most pliable of any of the special interest
> groups that we worked with.[7]

Later in the book, Martin cites the experience of James
Robinson, who stepped back from involvement with the
Religious Right because of his growing fear of what the
pursuit of power and the desire to be political power-
brokers could do to Christian leaders

> My motive started out pure, but power corrupts. Some
> people are terribly affected by it. I could have been. I
> found myself saying hard things about Jimmy Carter –
> hard, mean, cruel things. I found myself caught up in
> that, but the closer I got to it, I was frightened of it. I
> watched what it did to people. I watched how it fed,
> how it would drive them, to the point that I felt like
> principle could be sacrificed for power, even on the part

> of good, quality people. I thought, 'What is wrong with
> us?' And when I wanted to repent of all that, the
> Christian crowd that was supposed to be my friends got
> mad at me.

Testimonies like these make it all too clear just how dangerous and contaminating power can be, particularly to the Christian Church. Little wonder, then, that some would advise us to withdraw from such concerns and to devote all our attention to the 'spiritual work' of saving people's souls and preparing them for heaven. But that is always a mistake. The history of the acquiescence of much of the Christian church in the rise of Adolf Hitler and his Nationalist Socialist Party in Germany in the 1930s stands as a warning for all time that when we retreat from the public arena, an entire nation – indeed an entire world – can pay the price. The question is: can we find both a theology and a model of practice that will enable us to engage with integrity so that we can be salt and light in a world that is often marked by decay and darkness?

A different kind of Messiah

The beginnings of the answer to that question are found when we set the ministry of Jesus firmly within the context of life in first century Palestine. The history of the Jewish people prior to the birth of Christ is one long story of being ruled by a succession of foreign powers. In the middle of the second century BC, however, the Maccabean rebellion drove out the Greek occupying army and secured a hundred years of political freedom. But in 63 BC Palestine was once again over-run, this time by the Romans under the leadership of Pompey. The harshness of Roman rule was not tempered in any way by the puppet kings, who protected their own positions and lined their own pockets by doing the bidding of their imperial masters. The yoke of oppression was heavy on the people and inevitably there was a wave of apocalyptic and messianic expectation in first century Palestine: surely the new age that the prophets had dreamed of would break through; surely God's Messiah – the Anointed One – would end the reign of hated foreign oppressors. The messianic hope took different forms, sometimes envisaging a heavenly figure who would usher in the worldwide reign of God, at other times looking forward to a mighty warrior king whose military triumphs would set the people free.

And while they waited with varying degrees of expectancy for things to change, they had to find a way of living with Roman rule. In practice, there were really only four choices that could be made. For the great majority of ordinary people, it simply meant walking the path of *accommodation*. They were living in an occupied country with all the inevitable inconveniences that entailed. There was nothing that could be done and they simply had to accommodate themselves to it and make the best of things. Others, however, felt much more strongly. The Zealots were the militant terrorists of their day, who believed that slaying the enemies of God was a religious duty and that the longed-for messianic age would be brought about only by armed *rebellion*. But that was the last thing the religious hierarchy and the high priestly elite in Jerusalem wanted. Like many among the privileged and wealthy upper classes in every occupied land and in every age, they saw *collaboration* with the enemy as the only way to go to guarantee their survival. History records that the family of Annas, who held the office of high priest for most of the time from AD 6 to

AD 42, spent vast sums of money raised from the sale of animals for Temple sacrifices on bribes for Roman officials. And finally there were the Essenes, for whom the only answer to the political power and military threat of Rome was to withdraw into the *isolation* of religious communities, in which they pursued their faith and practised their piety in the alternative and purer culture of those who shared their creed and convictions.

Then, into this ferment of messianic expectation and competing ideologies of how to live as the people of God in an occupied country, stepped Jesus, the humble carpenter from Nazareth. While it is true, as has often been noted – for reasons that will become clear – that he avoided an open declaration of himself as Messiah early in his ministry, it is undeniable nonetheless that his message and ministry were unambiguously messianic. Just two incidents, one from early in his ministry and the other as it moved to its climax, put that fact beyond any possible doubt. There was the unforgettable day when he entered the synagogue in his home town, received the scroll of the prophet Isaiah and began to read from a passage that every devout Jew understood as a prophecy of the radical transformation that would be brought about by God's action through his Messiah

> The Spirit of the Lord is on me,
> because he has anointed me
> to preach good news to the poor.
> He has sent me to proclaim freedom for the prisoners
> and recovery of sight for the blind,
> to release the oppressed,
> to proclaim the year of the Lord's favour (Lk. 4:18,19).

You can almost feel the tension in the synagogue that day in Luke's terse description of what immediately followed the reading: 'Then he rolled up the scroll, gave it back to the attendant and sat down. The eyes of everyone in the synagogue were fastened on him and he began by saying to them, "Today this Scripture is fulfilled in your hearing"' (Lk. 4:20,21).

This is much more than 'local boy makes good'. This is nothing less than 'local boy lays claims to be the Messiah'! Such an incident could hardly go unnoticed and word of this latest claimant to the role of Messiah would soon have found its way to the authorities in Jerusalem.

Then there was the incident in the temple at Jerusalem in the days leading up to the cross (Lk. 19:45,46) where Jesus overturned the tables of the money-changers and threw out the traders who were selling animals for sacrifice. This was not simply a demonstration of his anger against the misuse of a place of prayer as an opportunity for the high priestly family to get rich at the expense of humble worshippers. Schooled as they were in the ancient Jewish scriptures, many of those present would have recalled the words of the prophet Malachi recorded some four hundred years earlier, when he spoke of the 'day of the Lord' and described his coming to his temple with all the fury of a refiner's fire (Mal. 3:1,2). The Pharisees and the teachers of the law would have recognised immediately that this was an act of deep symbolism and messianic significance.

No wonder that Jesus from Nazareth, like many other pretenders to the role of Messiah in Jewish history, ended up on a Roman cross. To make such a claim in words or in deeds was to risk your life, for it had both profoundly spiritual and provocatively political implications. To announce yourself as the Messiah, involving as it did a claim to be the agent of God's purposes in freeing his people, inevitably meant standing in opposition to the religious élite with their vested interest in maintaining the status quo and their policy of collaboration. And given the popular expectations that the Messiah would lead a rebellion against the occupying power, it would also be unpalatable to their Roman political masters. It is not difficult to see why Jesus fell foul of both and why he ended up on a cross. But in Jesus' case, there was even more to trouble the religious leaders in Jerusalem.

It wasn't simply that his manifesto was inescapably messianic; his ministry and his teaching differed from others who had made such a claim and they differed so radically that, if you took him seriously, they challenged not only your religious beliefs, but your relationship to your neighbours and to the state itself. Jesus spoke on matters of faith and conduct with an authority that his contemporaries had never encountered before. Early on in his ministry, when confronted by the paralytic who was brought by his four friends and lowered through the roof of a crowded house in Capernaum, his words went far beyond a promise of physical healing. He instructed the man to take up his bed and walk, but only after he had promised the sufferer lying in front of him, 'Son, your sins are forgiven (Mk. 2:1–12). The teachers of the law correctly observed that only God had the authority to do such a thing. Either this man was guilty of the worst kind of blasphemy or he was someone to be reckoned with, someone who held within him the authority of God himself.

What must have been equally disquieting to his hearers was the fact that he presented a startling alternative to the commonly accepted ways of dealing with relationships in general and with an oppressive occupying force in particular. Instead of the weary *accommodation* of the ordinary people, the armed *rebellion* of the Zealots, the self-interested *collaboration* of the religious élite or

the pious *isolation* of the Essenes, Jesus offered something much more costly but much more powerful. It was
a way that would not be content simply either to confront or tolerate evil, but to *transform* it – a way that had
the undreamed-of power and potential to change enemies into friends. It was a way – and this is surely why
Jesus was reluctant to declare himself as the Messiah in
so many words – that was very different from any of the
popular ideas of how the Messiah would fulfil his role;
if many were looking for someone who would wield the
sword in the destruction of their enemies, Jesus was not
that man! His was the way of the *suffering servant* depic-
ted in Isaiah's great poem that we looked at when we
considered Jesus' passion.

But it is essential at this point to understand that Jesus
embraced the concept of the suffering servant not just as
the reason for the cross but as the rationale for the whole
of life. In the face of all that we normally recognise as
power – whether personal, military or political – Jesus
embodied in his life and teaching a very different kind of
strength. It was neither weak nor passive; it did not simply give into oppressors or walk away from a fight; it
faced them head on with a dynamic that was active, loving and non-violent. Consider his words in what we
have come to call the Sermon on the Mount

> You have heard that it was said, 'Eye for eye, and tooth for
> tooth.' But I tell you, Do not resist an evil person. If some-
> one strikes you on the right cheek, turn to him the other
> also. And if someone wants to sue you and take your
> tunic, let him have your cloak as well. If someone forces
> you to go one mile, go with him two miles (Mt. 5:38–41).

Many of us have read or heard those words so often that
they now have a kind of pious ring to them; they've

become little more than the poetic expression of a virtuous ideal. They would have sounded very different to Jesus' original audience! His words about 'an eye for an eye and a tooth for a tooth' are quoted from the Old Testament Scriptures. And they represented a significant advance on the morality of the time in which they were written. The prevailing philosophy of that day was that, if someone did you wrong, you did something far worse to them. The teaching of an 'eye for an eye' is not a licence for revenge. Rather, it's a constraint on any punishment that could be exacted, a kind of statute of limitation, an insistence that the penalty suffered had to be proportionate to the crime committed. But Jesus goes far beyond that. His way is to come against the evil act in an entirely different manner, to accept the hurt but to meet it with a greater act of kindness.

And he applies it to every area of life. The blow on the cheek with the back of the hand was considered the worst of personal insults, like spitting on someone today. His instruction to 'turn the other cheek' is a dramatic way of saying that we must take the hurt that comes in personal relationships with an attitude that will accept pain, that will not exact revenge, that will not break the relationship and that will express itself in the kind of response that surprises the other person with love. His words about being sued for your tunic and allowing your adversary to take your cloak as well, indicate beyond doubt that he believed the same attitude should prevail in matters of business and commerce – a very different approach from the idea that winning is everything and profit is the bottom line.

Perhaps most disturbing of all to first century Jews would have been his encouragement to 'go the extra mile'. This was much more than merely a pious injunction to offer a little more service than is strictly necessary. It is nothing less than an insistence that the way of suffering servanthood applies in the arena of public affairs and political realities. The word in the original Greek text that is translated as 'force' in English is a technical, military term that means 'to press into service'. It is the same word that is used in Matthew 27:32 where Simon of Cyrene is made to carry the cross of Jesus on the way to Calvary. Jesus is proposing an entirely new way to relate to the hated Roman occupiers; it is a way that refuses to consign any group of people to the category of 'enemies', a way that embraces them as fellow human beings, a way that is costly and counter-intuitive, but ultimately full of possibilities for transforming and redeeming our thinking about power, our response to power and our use of power.

A different kind of procession

There is, of course, no greater example of this kind of power in action than the cross itself. And there is no more graphic presentation in the New Testament of what it means than Paul's daring and extravagant word-picture of the death of Jesus in his letter to the Colossian church. In one brief sentence he sums up the incredible victory of the cross: 'And having disarmed the powers and authorities, he made a public spectacle of them, triumphing over them (literally 'leading them in a triumphal procession') by the cross' (Col. 2:15).

The image in Paul's mind is that of the 'Roman Triumph', an event that was the crowning achievement for any Roman general who had been victorious over the enemies of Rome. To understand fully the daring irony of Paul's metaphor, we must have a picture of one of these imperial extravaganzas in our minds. On his return from battle, the military hero was allowed to lead his army in a victory procession within the gates of the imperial city and to display to his grateful fellow-citizens the defeated leaders, the captives who had been taken and any treasure that had been looted on the campaign. Designed both as political statements of the power of Rome and as religious acts of worship beseeching Jupiter, the ruler of all the gods and the patron god of Rome, to continue to make the Empire prosperous and successful, they were magnificent affairs.

At the head of the parade would be the members of the Senate, accompanied by trumpeters to announce their arrival; they would be followed by carts laden with the spoils of victory and behind them would come elephants, rare animals and exotic flora from the conquered land; then the arms and insignia of the defeated enemy would be carried in front of the enemy leaders themselves, closely followed by their relatives and other notable captives. Only now was the crowd that lined the route deemed ready to greet the victorious general himself, magnificently attired in a gold-embroidered robe, wearing a laurel wreath on his head, holding a laurel bough in his right hand and a sceptre in his left, riding in a circular chariot drawn by four horses and followed by his adult sons, his senior officers and the entire body of his infantry holding aloft laurel embroidered spears. To say that it was an impressive, even awe-inspiring, sight is to be guilty of understatement. The onlookers were certainly left in no doubt as to who were the winners and who were the losers.

Now look again at Paul's sentence summing up the truth of what happened on the cross. Instead of the conquered leaders of some nation that Rome had annexed and over-run, there are the 'powers and authorities', words that Paul uses to describe both the great societal, economic and political structures of human power (with all the injustice and oppression that so often infests them) and the great spiritual forces, created by God but fallen and corrupted, that undergird and help to shape them. Jesus is on the cross because of the vested interest of religious leaders and the compromised power of Pilate, the Roman Procurator who lacked the courage to resist their pressure. But he is also there because of the demonic forces that seek to stand against and to destroy all that is good and of God. Yet – and here's the daring irony of Paul's metaphor – like a victorious Roman general, Jesus is leading them in a triumphal procession.

The difference is that, instead of a military conqueror dressed in a gold-embroidered robe and riding in a chariot, the victor in this case is a young man pinned to a cross, writhing in agony, hung up like a side of meat, covered in a blanket of blood, sweat and flies, refusing to succumb to hate and praying for his executioners with his dying breath. It is a picture that is both ironic and insightful, terrible and beautiful in equal measure; and it is a very different kind of power from anything that is normally defined by that word. This is the power of a love that cannot be overcome by hatred, a love that forgives whatever the wrong that is done to it, a love that ultimately transforms a place of injustice into a place of redemption, a love that causes us to designate what seemed to be the darkest day in human history as *Good Friday*.

A different kind of certainty

It is, of course, a picture that leaves us with some big questions. How can we be sure that Jesus was right?

How can we be sure that the love Jesus demonstrated on the cross really does have the last word? How can we be sure that the abusive examples of power we see all around us are really living on borrowed time? How can we be sure that his death really is a victory and not a defeat? How can we be sure that Paul's picture of a triumphal procession is not merely the result of an overactive pious and poetic imagination? To those questions, there are two answers.

The first is that Jesus rooted his understanding of what it meant to be God's Messiah and how we should live as God's people, not simply in a sense that love is better than hate, but in the very nature of God himself. His conviction that we should love our enemies, that we should follow the path of suffering servanthood and that we should seek to transform every situation and overcome every manifestation of evil with good arose from the fact that he believed that *this is what his Father is like*. In all of human history there has never been anyone who was more tuned to the heart of God than Jesus and that fact gives his life and teaching an authority we find in no-one else. Listen again to his words on loving our enemies

> You have heard that it was said, 'Love your neighbour and hate your enemy.' But I tell you: Love your enemies and pray for those who persecute you, that you may be sons of your Father in heaven. He causes his sun to rise on the evil and the good, and sends rain on the righteous and the unrighteous. If you love those who love you, what reward will you get? Are not even the tax collectors doing that? And if you greet only your brothers, what are you doing more than others? Do not even pagans do that? Be perfect, therefore, as your heavenly Father is perfect (Mt. 5:43–48).

We can be sure of the power of love because the one man, who knew God better than any other person has ever done, assures us that love is the very heart of a God who showers his generous gifts on good and bad alike. And where other religions teach the power of moral rectitude as the ultimate expression of a godly life, Jesus says that the perfection to which we are called is a perfection of love for others.

The second answer to our questions is the answer of the empty tomb and the Risen Lord. If Jesus had been mistaken about the nature of God, his body would long since have decayed; his followers throughout the centuries might still have been stirred by the beauty of his life and teaching; we today might be among the millions who honour his memory and visit whatever shrine we believe to be the site of his last resting place. But things have taken a very different course. The excursions of the women to the empty tomb on the first Easter morning and the experiences of the disciples who encountered the Risen Lord in the days that followed – the same Jesus who was crucified, dead and buried – these have become the twin pillars on which our faith is founded and on which our certainty that he was right is securely fixed. The recurring refrain of the New Testament is that God raised Jesus from the dead, vindicated his life and his teaching, demonstrating beyond dispute that Jesus can be trusted and love has the victory. On such an answer, countless men and women of faith have risked everything and proved in their experience that it was a risk well worth taking.

Six

proof: embracing the mystery

It was back in the early Seventies, a time when you could still sing *Kumbaya* and not be greeted by a mixture of groans and derisory laughter; on reflection, people did sometimes laugh and jeer, but at least you could still get out alive! To be honest, I can't recall whether we really were singing *Kumbaya*. But I do know that, whatever the song was, it had to be possible to accompany it with only three chords, because that represented the furthest frontiers of our strictly limited musical abilities. However, we more than made up for our lack of musical sophistication with evangelistic fervour. 'Have guitar, will travel' was our motto, as we sallied forth into the streets of London with the good news of the gospel. And it was definitely 'in yer face' stuff. We sang loudly, testified fervently, preached passionately and argued vehemently. Where even two or three were gathered together on a street corner just minding their own business, there we were in the midst of them; if we didn't always manage to bless them, we did usually manage to attract their attention, at least for five minutes – which was all the time we needed to tell them that 'Jesus is the answer.'

At the end of these evangelistic sorties, we always returned home exhausted and more than a little hoarse, but quietly confident that we had fulfilled the Great Commission. At least, that was the case until the evening we took our evangelistic enterprise to Piccadilly Circus. In those days, long before the restricted access of today, literally hundreds of people would crowd onto the island in the middle of the road where the figure of Eros stands and the steps around the foot of the statue provided a perfect seating area. For us it was a dream come true – not just a crowd of people seated and comfortable, but a captive audience who could escape our singing and preaching only if they were willing to risk their lives by dashing through the busy London traffic that swirled around us. We'd never had such an opportunity. Usually our audience would move on after five minutes but these people were going nowhere quickly. So, after we'd addressed them en masse for half an hour or so, we split up and moved among them, delighted at the chance of one-on-one conversation.

It was then I met her – a young American woman – the second woman who would change my life! To avoid any misunderstanding, I ought to say that Margaret, my wife, and I had been happily married for a couple of years at this point and that the encounter at the statue of Eros – despite the setting – was definitely not a romantic one. This was a meeting that led, if not to a crisis of faith, then certainly to some serious questions about what I believed, why I believed those things and how I could share them with others.

I cannot any longer recall the details of my part in the conversation. No doubt I shared my testimony and witnessed to the fact that I believed that Jesus was the way, the truth and the life – the only way to the Father. It was her response to my certainties that took the wind out of my sails and shook my comfortable complacency. Her tone was courteous and her smile was sympathetic as she said, 'I respect you and what you're doing. I accept that Jesus is your way to find truth. You just need to respect the fact that I find my truth by a different route.'

With the hindsight of more than thirty years, the history of the New Age Movement, the prevailing philosophy of post-modern culture and the relativism that prevails today, her words now have a familiar ring. But back then, standing at the foot of the statue of Eros, it was the first time I had been forced to confront the question of how we apprehend and communicate truth, to face the fact that my well-rehearsed combination of rational argument and biblical proof texts were *of themselves* ineffective in bringing people to faith in Christ. I've never met that young American woman since that day, but if I ever did and if we recognised each other after all these years, I would thank her for what she did to set me on a journey that continues to this day as I wrestle with the mystery of faith and the challenge of sharing it with others.

Biblical authority

Of course, for all Christians – particularly those of us in the evangelical tradition – the Bible has a unique authority. It is, after all, the story of God's dealings with his people, the unfolding revelation of his character, the source of our knowledge of the life, death and resurrection of Jesus, the record of the Early Church and the basis for our knowledge of the teaching of the apostles. We believe, as Paul put it in his letter to Timothy, that 'All Scripture is God-breathed and is useful for teaching, rebuking, correcting and training in righteousness, so that the man of God may be thoroughly equipped for every good work' (2 Tim. 3:16.17).

Wherever there are followers of Jesus seeking to live out and communicate their faith to others, the Bible will have a place of primary importance. But – and this is vital to bear in mind when we are seeking to communicate with non-Christians – we too easily forget that the authority of the Bible is always a recognised authority, not an *imposed* authority. A brief backward glance at the history of the Church will make it clear what we mean by that.

In the early centuries of the Church, there were numerous collections of gospels and epistles which were used both in the instruction of new converts and in worship, alongside the Jewish Scriptures that we now know as the Old Testament. Eusebius of Caesarea, a Church historian living in the fourth century AD, divided these writings into three groups – those that were universally acknowledged throughout the Church, those that were disputed and those that were spurious or heretical. The latter category clearly threatened both the unity of the Church and the orthodoxy of belief, so it was important for gatherings of Church leaders, such as the Council of Laodicea in 363 AD, to decide on what books should be accepted as part of the official *canon* (a Greek word that literally means a 'measuring stick') of Scripture. In doing so, their decisions as to what to include and what to leave out were based on three criteria: the writings in question had to conform to the accepted teaching of the Church in its credal statements; they had to be of apostolic origin, either written by or containing the teaching of one of the apostles; and they had to be already in use in the churches. It is clear from these principles that the great historic councils were not *imposing* Scripture on the churches; rather, they were simply *recognising* those sacred writings whose God-breathed authority was already generally accepted.

Consequently, when we echo the cry of the Protestant Reformation, *Sola Scriptura* – 'Scripture alone is our authority', it is not quite as simple as we sometimes imagine. The existence of a multitude of denominations is evidence enough that equally sincere people can interpret the same biblical passages in very different ways. Too often we have taken the authority of Scripture to mean that it's everyone for themselves with a Bible. The truths of Scripture, however, need to be reflected upon within the community of the church, with due respect to the teachings and tradition of the Church and with enough humility on the part of each one of us to acknowledge that, while God has spoken with authority in his word, we, in our frailty and imperfection, are capable of misunderstanding and misapplying that word.

It is equally important when we share our faith with others that we allow them to recognise the authority of Scripture rather than that we seek to impose it upon them. It's a lesson I have learned again in recent days. Here in Manchester, where I live, the churches have been working with the Bible Society in a Bible advocacy campaign. We've used everything from enormous advertising hoardings to beer mats and taxis to publicise the Bible as relevant and accessible. I'm sure that a great deal of good has been achieved as churches and organisations have worked together with our partners in the Bible Society in organising events around the central promotion. But research subsequent to the campaign has shown that whilst we stimulated renewed interest in the Bible among lapsed Christians, we actually managed to annoy people who had no faith and no link with church. On reflection – and it's always easy with hindsight – it appears most likely that this happened because, in our enthusiasm, we made one fatal change of course midway through the planning. Originally we were going to build the campaign around the theme of 'homecoming'; we wanted to touch on things that mattered to everyone – home, family, acceptance – and then help them to see how their deepest concerns were echoed and answered in the Bible; we were on track to encourage them to discover and recognise its authority for themselves.

For various reasons, however, we changed the approach. Our slogan became 'The Riddle of Life' and we used some provocative questions in the form of very slick and clever headlines that linked back to biblical passages. It was no-one's fault and we all share the responsibility, but, without realising it until it was too late, we had lapsed back into the paradigm of imposing authority. We were telling them that the Bible had the answers and they weren't even interested in the questions we had chosen. We meant well, but we missed an opportunity. We weren't the first to make that mistake. And we make it every time we refer to the Bible as 'the Maker's handbook'. I know why we do it, but it really is not a helpful way to describe Scripture. It's hard to think of anything less exciting or more unattractive. The only time anyone turns to the manufacturer's manual is when something goes wrong; and, although women are much more sensible about such things, men regard it as some kind of defeat if they can't work it all out without referring to the instructions! For followers of Jesus, of course, the Bible will always be the divine rule of faith and practice; but for non-believers there is nothing that is less likely to encourage them to discover the authority of the God-breathed contents of the Bible than this kind of approach.

Doctrinal integrity

The question that faces us then is this: how do we express the truths of the Bible in such a way that they can be encountered and understood not only by those within the Church but also by those with whom we want to share our faith? One obvious answer is that we do so in our creeds and in our doctrinal statements. For many of us, they have been the foundational non-negotiables of our faith. Often, when we seek to work together with Christians of different traditions, assent to such statements is seen as the basis of our unity; conversely, an inability to agree on a shared declaration of our beliefs prevents us from engaging in mutual worship and witness. Clearly there is sound logic behind this kind of approach. There has to be an 'irreducible minimum' on which Christians need to agree. It makes no sense to believe just anything and imagine that you can label it as 'Christian'. But the matter of 'sound doctrine' is not quite as simple as it first appears.

Theology is not the same as 'the faith once and for all delivered to the saints'. The *faith* is primary: it is the belief that God has acted uniquely in and through Jesus Christ and the resulting commitment of all that we are to that conviction. Theology and the development of doctrine represent a vital but secondary activity; they are our intellectual reflection on and our attempt to articulate what God has revealed in the Bible and through Jesus. The ancient credal statements of the Church – such as the Apostles' Creed or the Nicene Creed – are foundational examples of this. Because they hold so much of the accumulated wisdom of the Church throughout the centuries, we rightly give great weight to them. They stand like great doctrinal signposts to guide us as we seek to apprehend the essentials of our faith.

But even here we need to be careful and we do well to heed the wise counsel of Stanley J. Grenz

> The assumption of an unaltered corpus of doctrine artic-
> ulated for all time by the Christians of the early centuries,
> while in a sense true, nevertheless oversimplifies a com-
> plex phenomenon. All expressions of the faith, including
> the early creeds and all claimants to the status of being
> the eternal corpus of doctrine, are culturally conditioned.
> They were formulated in the linguistic and philosophical
> frameworks of the age in which they were written.
> Consequently, our understanding of the heritage of the
> church as a norm for theology must be nuanced.[8]

The implications of Grenz's words must not be lost on us. All theology and all statements of doctrine are important insofar as they safeguard the great truths of the gospel. But all theology and all statements of doc-trine are conditioned by the time and culture in which they are articulated; that is their limitation and their jus-tification – they express unchanging gospel truth for that time, place and culture. And each one of us, to a greater or lesser extent, has to do the hard work of 'being the-ologians' as we explore what we believe, discern how those beliefs are integrated into our lives and discover how to share those truths with others in a way that is intelligible and attractive. Theology must always give birth to apologetics – the reasoned defence and explana-tion of our faith to non-believers.

Personal spirituality

Our statements of doctrine – whether the great credal statements of the church or our own personal efforts to communicate our faith in words at the office water-cooler or over the garden fence – are neither the proof of the gospel nor the essence of our faith. Because they are the result of our human reasoning on God's revelation, they will often contain aspects of our own misunder-standings as much as they encapsulate gospel truth. To return to our analogy above, they are at best signposts to guide us and keep us on the right path as followers of Jesus; but they are not the path itself. To paraphrase St Paul's famous words in his first letter to the church at Corinth, even if we could fathom all the mysteries of faith and articulate all the wonders of God's revelation but we lack love, it will all amount to nothing. The real-ity of our faith can never be fully encapsulated in any formula of words, however wise and however correct.

We should not be surprised by that, for at the heart of the gospel is the assertion that even God himself would not trust his revelation to words alone. The supreme insight of the prologue to John's gospel is that God chose to incarnate his grace and truth in the life of Jesus, that 'the word of God became a human being and lived among us. We saw his splendour (the splendour as of a father's only son), full of grace and truth' (Jn.1:14).[9] He still chooses to work in the same way through our imperfect lives; if his grace and truth are not to some extent incarnate in us, then all our efforts at presenting or explaining the gospel will be futile. There must always be, as we have said, a place for *apologetics* – the reasoned defence of our faith. But there is a greater need for an *embodied apologetic*. Our lives must be the most effective argument for the reality and relevance of the gospel. People will not believe the truths we declare unless we live in such a way that it makes those truths credible. Biblical authority and doctrinal integrity must 'become flesh' in us.

When the Revised Version of the Bible was published in 1855 there were many scholarly comments made by clergy and academics. But perhaps no-one was more perceptive in their remarks than William Booth. He wrote to the officers and soldiers in his Salvation Army, encouraging them to avail themselves of this new resource and describing its publication as 'the event of the past week'. But he went on to make two observations which could only come from someone with his heart for mission. He lamented the fact that the language was still archaic and said that he would have been happier if the translation had been rendered 'not in the stiff and ancient language used three hundred years ago, but in the form of speech employed by the present day'. Then he concluded his article by challenging his readers as to where the real work of translation and application of biblical truth always has to be done: 'If the Revision throws any new light upon the precious volume – the Book of books – I shall accept it very gratefully. Meanwhile . . . I want to see *a new translation of the Bible* into the hearts and conduct of living men and women . . . It is no use making correct translations of the words if we cannot get the words translated into life.'[10]

Alternative community

Booth was right, of course and his emphasis on mission and holy living continue to challenge us. But, like many an evangelist since, his passion to reach the lost and to call for personal commitment to Christ sometimes led him to undervalue the importance of the Church as a visible alternative community in which the new relationships of the gospel – the relationship with the Father through Jesus in the Spirit and the relationship with each other as brothers and sisters in Christ – are demonstrated to a watching, fractured, divided world. It is ironic that it so easily escapes our notice that an *embodied apologetic* can be fully expressed only through the Church, the Body of Christ on earth.

We so often rightly remind each other that 'the church is not the building, but the people'. We're not wrong to say that; the problem is that we seem to think that, when we've said that, we've said everything. We need to go beyond that truism and remind ourselves that 'the church' is far more than a few hundred people met for a Sunday service and that membership of the church means far more than signing our agreement to a statement of doctrine, far more than giving up eight or ten hours a week to be involved in Bible studies, cell groups, choir practices, prayer meetings or even well-intentioned community activities, far more than tithing our income to the fellowship to which we belong. Being the church – *really being the church* – means committing ourselves to a company of believers, seeking an intimacy with them and with God and, paradoxically, expressing that intimacy through a welcoming openness to anyone and everyone who is attracted by the quality of our corporate life.

We need to go further still. We need to acknowledge that the time we spend 'in church' will – for all of us apart from the 'full-time' paid staff – always be just a fraction of our waking hours. I find myself in agreement with a friend of mine who always pleads that we should call our gatherings for worship 'meetings' rather than 'services'. His rationale is simple. 'The service only begins,' he insists, 'when the meeting ends and we walk out through the door of the church.' I don't want for one minute to minimise the importance of the time we spend in corporate worship. I say 'amen' as loudly as anyone when the preacher quotes Hebrews 10:25: 'Let us not give up meeting together, as some are in the habit of doing . . .' But I also want to raise my hand and point out the context of that sentence. Immediately before it we are encouraged to 'consider how we may spur one another on towards love and good deeds' (v24) and immediately following it the writer highlights one of the purposes of our meeting together – to 'encourage one another' (v25b). In worship, the *gathered church* focuses on the grace and love of God so that the *dispersed church* is inspired and equipped to express that grace and love in the world of work and everyday living.

There are significant implications when we see the church in this way. It means that our relationship with Christ and with each other is not intended to hold us within the walls of the sanctuary, within the company of believers, or within the sub-culture of church activities. Instead, it is intended to inspire and equip us to move out into the world, in the knowledge that we are being supported by the invisible but powerful fellowship of our brothers and sisters in Christ who are upholding us with their love, their faith and their prayers. This in turn means that we need to avoid the temptation to judge the commitment of those brothers and sisters purely by the amount of time they spend in specifically church activities. In fact, we need to recognise that it may very well be more important for them to share a meal with a non-Christian neighbour, to attend a meeting of the local residents' association, to be present at a trades union meeting, or any one of a thousand things, than to be at a church event. To press the case even further, we may well need to re-imagine our churches and to restructure church activities precisely in order to free up our people to be the Body of Christ in the world. We will certainly need to look again at our preaching and teaching to ensure that it really does equip and enable our people to face the demands and answer the questions that the world will ask of them.

Embracing mystery

In ways such as these we will present the gospel to a watching world. But I am still troubled by the question of the young American woman at Piccadilly Circus. My evangelical upbringing instructs me that I should have told her that truth is absolute and not relative, that Jesus alone is the way, the truth and the life and that any other road to God is at best incomplete and at worst a dangerous blind alley that leads to delusion and destruction. But somehow I've grown less and less comfortable with that pat answer over the years. It isn't that I doubt for a moment that Jesus is the full and perfect revelation of God. It isn't that my respect for Scripture has grown less; if anything, I have a higher view of the Bible than ever. It isn't that I have rejected the great credal statements of the Church; they remain indispensable signposts on the road of faith. And it certainly isn't that I am wavering in my growing sense that the gospel is most credible and convincing when it is embodied in the individual lives of followers of Jesus and in the corporate life of the Church.

It's just that, firstly, I'm not as comfortable in dismissing her experience as I once was; she may be in a very different place from where I am, her path to faith may have taken many a wrong turning and she may still be a long way from commitment to Jesus. But, equally, she may have had a genuine encounter with God at some time, even if she lacked the theology and the insights of Scripture to help her understand it and interpret its meaning properly. And she – and all the folk like her I have met over the years – is my fellow-traveller on the road of life. Surely we should be able to have some point of contact, some area that we can share and discuss. And secondly and just as importantly, while I believe as passionately as ever that 'Jesus is the answer' to the world's needs, I am much less certain than I used to be that, simply because I am a Christian, I have *all the answers* to *every question*. I, too, have to live with a sense of mystery in my encounters with the living God.

John Humphrys, one of the presenters of Radio 4's *Today* programme, is typical of so many people in our society. He is unable to describe himself as a believer, but neither is he satisfied with the militant atheism of the kind peddled by Richard Dawkins. Humphrys has long been profoundly conscious of the awesome mystery of life and the questions raised by such an awareness. In his book, provocatively and appropriately entitled *In God we doubt*, he writes of the first stirrings of that consciousness

> I still recall the exact times and places when the Big Questions declared themselves to my childish consciousness. The first arrived when I was in short trousers and knew even less than I know today.
>
> I had been playing with some friends on a disused aerodrome near my home in Cardiff. We used the abandoned carcasses of old aircraft to attack the squadrons of imaginary German bombers droning above us in the darkening sky. When we had wiped them out, my friends went home for tea. I hung around. It was one of those days when my mother, a hairdresser who worked from home, was giving a perm to a neighbour and I hated the stench of the chemicals.
>
> By now it was dark. The glory of the night sky had yet to be lost to light pollution and on cloudless nights the

stars went on for ever. That was what troubled me. How could they go on for ever? And if the universe was everything, what was it all in? And how could it be in anything because that would have to be in something else and . . . and . . . and so on. And what was there before any of it existed? And how did it all come into existence? And finally – the really, really Big Question – why . . .

It took me a few more years to grasp that rather a lot of people were worrying about their own versions of the Big Questions and had been for quite a long time.[11]

In 2006 he hosted a series of three radio programmes entitled *Humphrys in search of God*, in which he interviewed the Archbishop of Canterbury, Dr. Rowan Williams; the Chief Rabbi, Sir Jonathan Sacks; and the highly respected Muslim academic and author, Tariq Ramadan. The fact that the series not only won a prestigious broadcasting award, but also attracted unexpectedly high listening figures and an unprecedented audience reaction, made it plain that Humphrys' search for faith touched something deep in the psyche of a nation often assumed to be entirely secular. John Humphrys has still not come to faith in Christ or even, for that matter, to a definite belief in God; but his words elsewhere in the book make it clear beyond any doubt that he, too, has sensed that terrible beauty that reason can neither explain nor explain away, that terrible beauty that is seen whenever goodness meets evil and suffering, that terrible beauty that we know to be displayed in all its perfect and wonderful fullness at Calvary

We each make our own choices.

One choice is to accept the conclusion reached by Jean-Paul Sartre in *The Age of Reason*: "There is no purpose to existence, only nothingness."

That is a perfectly rational conclusion if, like me, you cannot accept that we exist in order to worship God. It is very hard to see any purpose in a world where an accident of birth determines whether a child leads a long and healthy life or dies an early death in grinding poverty; a world of hunger and war and disease; a world that we may be destroying through our own greed and stupidity. But however much he may appeal to our reason, Sartre's conclusion is too bleak for me.

Trite it may be, but most of us can see the beauty as well as the horrors of the world and, sometimes, humanity at its most noble. We sense a spiritual element in that nobility and, in the miracle of unselfish love and sacrifice, something beyond our conscious understanding. You don't need to be an eastern mystic or a devout religious believer to feel that. We should not – we must not – be browbeaten by arrogant atheists and meekly accept their "deluded" label. They are no more capable of understanding this most profound mystery than a small child making his first awe-inspiring discoveries.

The point I want to make at the conclusion of this chapter is this: ultimately, we cannot 'prove' the reality of our faith, at least not in the way that we normally use that word. All of the really important things in life are beyond that kind of proof. I cannot 'prove' to you that my wife will love me, come what may; I cannot 'prove' to you that a piece of music is beautiful; I cannot 'prove' to you that the Bible is the written record of God's self-revelation to humanity; I cannot 'prove' to you that the death of Jesus is the ultimate reality from which everything else derives its meaning; indeed, the philosophers tell us that it is difficult even to 'prove' the reality of our own existence. All of these things have to be experienced and encountered and then, as John Humphrys says, we each make our own choices.

I become increasingly convinced that the primary task of the Church and of every individual follower of Jesus in our day is not to persuade people to assent to a series of doctrinal propositions; neither is it to provide the answers to whatever rational difficulties keep people from faith; nor is it to promote social policies and legislative agendas that reflect the convictions of Christians as to what is best for our society. All of those things have their place and must absorb our attention and our energies at times. But our primary task is to tell the story of the terrible beauty of the cross, to live it out whenever we confront suffering and evil and to help those around us – those who share our faith, those of other faiths and those who as yet have nothing they would describe as faith – to recognise that God – the God who loves us enough to send his Son to die for us – is with us in the best and the worst of times, in the terrible beauty of our human struggle with pain, suffering and evil, even when we do not know his name and only dimly recognise his presence.

Seven

poverty: practising the paradox

I am all too familiar with the deprivation and relative poverty of many inner city areas, both in Britain and in North America. And I have witnessed at first hand the absolute grinding poverty of the developing world in the shanty-towns of Africa and on the dusty streets of India. Such sights never cease to fill me with a mixture of anger, shame and compassion. But nothing has ever stirred me more deeply than Bob Geldof's description of his visit to the refugee camp at Mekele in Ethiopia, back in the 1980s. If you ever wondered why a rock star, whose chief concern had previously been where he'd find the next chart-hit, has stuck doggedly to the task of campaigning for the poor and hungry, the answer lies in experiences such as this

> This was a camp run by several organisations including the Red Cross. Round the edges were tens of thousands of people without any shelter. Towards the middle were rows upon rows of Army surplus-style tents sent from all over the world. In the centre were the Red Cross buildings for the worst cases . . . it reminded me of films I'd seen of Auschwitz . . .

Everything horrified me. Rows upon rows of people had each been given a handful of seeds which they were roasting in wok-type pans over tiny fires. They did not have the water to turn them into porridge. Water supplies were rationed. Firewood was getting more and more scarce. There were 50,000 people here and more arriving every day. This place was hot too and the tents buzzed with flies and disease. There were camp guards employed to try to prevent it, but people would just piss and shit anywhere. Many of them had such awful intestinal diseases (from contaminated water and from the hard grain which tore at the stomach) that they had no control over their bodily functions. It was in this camp that I had forced upon me one of the images which has haunted me ever since.

I came out of the long huts and saw a small boy squatting by a pool of his own urine and diarrhoea. He looked about four months old but malnutrition is deceptive. He was nearer two, the age of my own child in England. A tattered dusty piece of cotton hung from one shoulder across his distended stomach. His face was huge, a two-year-old face on a four-month-old body. His eyes were moons of dust and flies. He was crying and the tears rolled down to the awful swollen stomach before they dried in the heat. Only a few yards away were his family, but they were too ill to notice. The diarrhoea trickled out in a steady flow. Then, as I stood there, as I watched, the child began to shit out his own intestines. He had nothing left inside to evacuate except the torn shreds of his own stomach which had been ripped open by dry grain. I was watching a child die. There can be no doubt that the little boy is dead now. But he will not die in my imagination. There, nothing can free him from the agonising process of death which is fixed in my mind.[12]

I have two emotions as I copy that passage and type it into my computer. One is utter, desperate sadness that such poverty could exist – and still does exist – in our world. The other is fear – fear that some readers will be more offended by Geldof's blunt Anglo-Saxon words to describe the boy's bodily functions than they will be by the terrible obscenity of a child dying in agony from the effects of malnutrition. The time is long overdue for us to confront the issue: there is no greater evil than allowing millions of our fellow human beings to starve in a world where we in the West eat so much that we have made obesity one of the most common diseases of our generation and turned fad diets into a major industry. And that is just one aspect of our unthinking affluence in the face of the degrading poverty of the two-thirds world.

The reality

The reality is that the two-year-old boy Bob Geldof watched in the Mekele refugee camp is just one of millions in our world who live and die in abject poverty. The facts and figures have been put forward in numerous presentations and publications. They are so overwhelming as to leave us almost numb. Somewhere around 2.5 billion people live on less than two dollars a day, half of them on less than one dollar; fifteen thousand men and women die daily from diseases that could be prevented by clean water and basic medical care; the richest fifth of the world's population enjoy an income that is 74 times higher than the poorest fifth; one hundred million children, 58 million of them girls, have no school education; and – perhaps the statistic that highlights most starkly the hideous inequality of the world in which we live – it has been calculated that there are three billionaires whose combined assets are equivalent to that of the six hundred million poorest people on this planet! We could fill page after page with statistics like these, but the shocking truth is clear even from the few we have listed.

But even the presentation of such facts can leave us blind to the all-consuming nature of such desperate poverty. From our position of comfort, we can easily imagine that poverty simply means a low income and a lack of all of life's luxuries and many of its necessities. But those who have studied the situation closely are forced to use the phrase 'multiple poverty'. The world's poor are utterly vulnerable. They are at the front-line of the devastating effects of climate change – deforestation, drought, flooding – things that we inaccurately describe as 'natural disasters'. The real truth is that, when these events take place, the poor are literally paying the price – in many cases with their lives – of our thoughtless pillaging of the world's limited resources. And they are defenceless against an entire catalogue of calamities that follow in the wake of dire poverty – illiteracy, malnutrition, high infant mortality rates, low life expectancy, crime, government corruption, war, powerlessness and exposure to disease.

Nothing demonstrates the all-pervading evil influence of poverty more than the worldwide AIDS pandemic. There are more than forty million people who carry the HIV virus or who have full-blown AIDS, but over ninety per cent of them live in developing countries and the effects are devastating. In Europe and North America people who are HIV positive have ready access to retroviral drugs that can keep them not only alive but also healthy for many years. In Africa and Asia, however, those with the disease are dying because they are too poor to afford the treatment that is so readily available to the wealthy. (Of course, as is often argued, there are cultural factors and issues of sexual behaviour that need to be addressed, but those things must not blind us to the fact that poverty is the primary factor in the terrible and stubborn hold of the disease in poor countries.) Some twenty million people have already died from AIDS and there are estimated to be fifteen million AIDS orphans in developing countries. An entire generation is being lost – those who would be the labourers, leaders, doctors, civil servants – and the result is that poverty takes an even stronger grip as entire economies grind to a halt. In just one African country, Zambia, approximately half the teachers being trained each year are dying from AIDS.

There is no denying that much of the responsibility for such poverty lies with corrupt leaders, ineffective governments and warring factions in some of these countries. But that is certainly not the whole picture. In recent years, the wealthier nations have at last begun to address the issue of international debt which has been a major factor in keeping countries poor. But there is much that remains to be done and there are still developing countries that are forced to spend more on the repayment of loans than on their health services. There are also issues surrounding international trade that need to be addressed; the rules are often weighted in favour of the richer countries, making it difficult for poorer nations to access international markets and sell their goods at fair prices; trans-national corporations have been guilty of practices in developing countries – low wages, unsafe health and safety and environmental practices – that would never be tolerated in the developed world; and we, the consumers, expect and demand food and clothing at prices which deprive producers of a basic living wage. The bottom line on world poverty is that there is no one simple answer and that we all share the responsibility for the injustice that consigns millions of our fellow human beings to a level of subsistence that we ourselves would find totally unacceptable.

The theology

There is no excuse for us remaining indifferent to poverty. Even before we come to the teaching of Jesus and the Early Church, the Old Testament has a great deal to say on the subject. A brief overview of its pages will make it clear just how closely a proper response to poverty is linked to a true understanding of the nature of God and his purposes for the nation he had chosen. First and foremost, the calling of God's people to care for the poor was *rooted in Israel's salvation history*. They must give justice to the poor and oppressed because God had rescued *them* out of poverty and oppression in Egypt

> Do not ill-treat an alien or oppress him, for you were aliens in Egypt.
> Do not take advantage of a widow or an orphan. If you do and they cry out to me, I will certainly hear their cry . . .
> Do not deny justice to your poor people in their law-suits . . .
> Do not oppress an alien; you yourselves know how it feels to be aliens, because you were aliens in Egypt.
> (Ex. 22:21–23; 23:6,9)

Consequently, caring for the poor and oppressed was *enshrined in Israel's laws*. Lying in a court of law, accepting bribes, showing partiality in judgements, oppressing the poor in any way – all of these were forbidden on pain of the severest penalties. But even more significant were the numerous positive commands to act in ways that would alleviate poverty: interest was not to be charged on loans; poor people who sold themselves into slavery had to be released after seven years; debts had to be cancelled after a similar interval of time; slaves seeking refuge should not be handed back to their owners; when fields were harvested, some of the produce should always be left for 'the alien, the fatherless and the widow'; workmen were to be paid regularly and fairly; every third year a tenth of all agricultural produce was to be given to the poor. There was a bias to the poor built into Israel's laws.

Not surprisingly, this same principle was *proclaimed by Israel's prophets*. It might have been acceptable in the countries and cultures that surrounded Israel for powerful people to do as they pleased, but the prophets fearlessly reminded the nation that, whatever strata of society you belonged to, you were under the authority of Israel's God. And nothing angered God more than powerful people oppressing the poor. Two dramatic encounters – that of the prophet Nathan with King David after David had arranged the murder of Uriah and Elijah's challenge to King Ahab following the king's seizure of Naboth's vineyard – graphically demonstrate that even kings are subject to God's law on this matter. And Amos had no hesitation in addressing the upper-class women who 'oppress the poor and crush the needy' as 'you cows of Bashan'. Clearly he felt their lack of care for the underprivileged merited the strongest censure.

And when the prophets pointed to the hope of the Anointed One who would come as God's agent to free his people, they predicted that justice for the poor would be *embodied in Israel's Messiah*. Isaiah predicted that 'the Spirit of the Lord will rest on' the Messiah and that 'with righteousness he will judge the needy, with justice he will give decisions for the poor of the earth' (Isa. 11:2–4). The ancient seers believed that justice and equality for the poor were intrinsic to God's will being done in the world. The Messiah would be the Deliverer of the poor.

Inevitably the theme of God's concern for the poor was *expressed in Israel's worship*. John Stott has aptly and memorably described the Psalms as 'the hymn-book of the helpless'. Psalm 83 is a perfect example of exactly what he means. The psalmist presents a vision of God presiding in the great Hall of Justice in heaven, sur-rounded by judges and rulers whom he has called to give an account of how they have dispensed justice, par-ticularly to the poor and oppressed. As the people of Israel sang or recited these words, they would be left in no doubt as to God's heart on this matter

> God presides in the great assembly;
> he gives judgement among the "gods":
> "How long will you defend the unjust
> and show partiality to the wicked? . . .
> Defend the cause of the weak and fatherless;
> maintain the rights of the poor and oppressed.
> Rescue the weak and the needy;
> deliver them from the hand of the wicked . . ."
>
> (Ps. 82:1–4).

And when they were not praising God for his attitude to the poor, they were praying, in their poverty, that he would act on their behalf

> Rescue me, O Lord, from evil men;
> protect me from the men of violence . . .

> I know that the Lord secures justice for the poor
> and upholds the cause of the needy
>
> (Ps. 140:1,12).

For Israel, worship and praise were never an escape from the cause of a just society and the care of the poor. Rather, their 'hymn-book for the helpless' gave expression to those priorities and rejoiced in the fact that they were also God's priorities.

When we turn to the New Testament, the same concern is immediately evident in the Early Church. In his brief summary of life among the believers in Jerusalem towards the end of Acts chapter 2, Luke refers to the characteristics of the young Church – to the breaking of bread, to the apostles' teaching, to signs and wonders and to the numbers being added to the Church daily; but he is also careful to mention that the reality of their faith was also seen in the fact that some sold their possessions in order to release money so that those in need were cared for. Just a few chapters later (ch. 6), he relates the story of the restructuring of the Church's leadership in order to ensure that the Greek-speaking widows were properly cared for in the distribution of food.

Further on in the New Testament, this practical concern for the poor goes beyond the boundaries of the local church. For the church at Jerusalem subsequently fell on hard times and Paul made it his business to raise money on his missionary travels to support the mother church. There is no clearer indication of how central this was in his thinking than the opening words of the sixteenth chapter of his first letter to the Corinthian church. Having dealt with such lofty topics as church discipline, the place of spiritual gifts and the reality and nature of the resurrection, he immediately he goes on to say, without a hint of embarrassment or incongruity, 'Now about the collection for God's people . . .' (I Cor. 16:1), before listing some of the practical arrangements for receiving and passing on the money to the needy recipients.

We could go on quoting chapter and verse, but we can sum up the Bible's teaching on poverty in this way: there is little in the nature of a developed theology of poverty in the sense of the writers speculating on the reasons for its existence. They simply accept the fact that in a fallen and imperfect world, poverty is an ever-present reality. But they are far from fatalistic in their attitude to it. Instead, they see it as the duty of God's people, not only to act charitably and to give alms to the poor, but also to structure society in such a way that the worst effects of poverty are eliminated or at least alleviated. And the reason for their attitude is their belief that the God who acted to rescue Israel out of poverty and slavery in Egypt is the God who always cares for the poor, who intervenes on their behalf and who calls his people to reflect his character in their active concern for those in need.

The irony

When we come to the New Testament and to the ministry of Jesus, we encounter an irony in his teaching regarding poverty. There is no lessening of the insistence that poverty is an evil that God opposes and that we should do all we can to combat it. As we have seen in an earlier chapter, his 'Messiah's manifesto', delivered in the synagogue at Nazareth, committed him to a ministry of preaching 'good news to the poor'. His healing miracles – such as restoring sight to Bartimaeus in Mark chapter 10 – did more than set people free from sickness; in a society where there was no equivalent of our welfare state, healing the sick also liberated them from poverty and from the need to beg. His disgust at the behaviour of the wealthy guests, at a dinner-party given by a prominent Pharisee, prompted Jesus to remind them of the nature of true hospitality and of their responsibility to the poor.

> When you give a luncheon or dinner, do not invite your friends, your brothers or relatives, or your rich neighbours; if you do, they may invite you back and so you will be repaid. But when you give a banquet, invite the poor, the crippled, the lame, the blind, and you will be blessed. Although they cannot repay you, you will be repaid at the resurrection of the righteous (Lk. 14:12–14).

Not surprisingly, as the One who came to fulfil the Old Testament Scriptures, Jesus sees the poor as being of special concern to his Father and, consequently, particularly deserving of our care. We should not misunderstand his rebuke to the disciples for their criticism of the woman who poured the expensive perfume over him. When he responded that 'the poor you will always have with you' (Mt. 26:11) he was not providing them with an excuse for complacency. Rather he was reminding them of the hard reality of life and providing them with an incentive for ongoing, open-hearted generosity.

But Jesus also understands something else from his Jewish Scriptures: the poor have both a special place in God's heart and a heightened awareness of their reliance on God. Unlike the rich and powerful who are tempted to think that they can live to themselves, the poor know that their hope is in God alone. So again and again in the Psalms, the word 'poor' almost becomes a synonym for devotion to God and holy living. The link between poverty and piety is nowhere more clearly expressed than in Psalm 34:

I sought the LORD, and he answered me;
he delivered me from all my fears.
Those who look to him are radiant:
their faces are never covered with shame.
This poor man called, and the LORD heard him;
he saved him out of all his troubles.
The angel of the LORD encamps around those who fear
    him,
and he delivers them (Ps. 34:4–7).

This embryonic Old Testament principle – the poor understand their need of God – is birthed and brought fully to life in the irony at the heart of Jesus' teaching: *It remains true that we must work to eliminate, or at least to alleviate, poverty; but it is equally true that we must willingly embrace it and resist the seductive power of money and possessions.* The most obvious reason for this call to embrace poverty is to be found in the effect that riches have on those who hold them. The possession of great wealth is spiritually dangerous and there are two places in the gospels where this is highlighted. One is in the response of Jesus to an appeal made to him to mediate in a dispute between two brothers regarding their inheritance. He refused to act as arbiter and took the opportunity to warn the crowd around him: 'Watch out! Be on your guard against all kinds of greed; a man's life does not consist in the abundance of his possessions' (Lk. 12:15).

But as usual, Jesus preferred to cast the truth in the drama of a parable, rather than in the dull dogma of a principle and he went on to relate the story of the rich farmer whose land produced such a good crop that he resolved to tear down his existing barns to make way for larger storage facilities. The man's entire philosophy of life is summed up in his brief soliloquy: 'This is what I'll do. I will tear down my barns and build bigger ones and there I will store all my grain and my goods. And I'll say to myself, 'You have plenty of good things laid up for many years. Take life easy; eat, drink and be merry' (Lk. 12:18,19).

There is not the slightest hint in Jesus' story that the farmer had amassed his wealth by anything other than honest effort. And yet, for all that, God calls him a fool and his days on earth come to an abrupt and sudden end. As the audience reflected on the story they would understand why: this man had been lulled into a sense of false security by his wealth. His lack of understanding of his true situation had three consequences. He lacked any sense of *God's generosity towards him*; there is not a word of gratitude for God's creation or the processes of nature through which his wealth came, or the God-given skills that made him so successful. He lacked any sense of his *responsibility towards others*; just notice how often the personal pronoun occurs in his speech and how his whole concern is for his own comfort. And he lacked any sense of *his own mortality*; he assumes that he will live for ever and forgets that life on earth is not permanent. In short, despite his material wealth – or probably more accurately, because of it – he is 'not rich towards God' (Lk. 12:21). And those four words highlight one of the great dangers of riches – they distract us from the things that are really important.

The other episode that springs to mind is, of course, the encounter of Jesus with the wealthy young aristocrat who wanted to know how he could inherit eternal life. On being reminded of the commandments, he is able to unhesitatingly respond that he has observed them all since boyhood. So Jesus confronts him with a challenge that goes right to the heart of his problem: 'You still lack one thing. Sell everything you have and give to the poor and you will have treasure in heaven. Then come, follow me' (Lk. 18:22).

This is not a story with a happy ending, alas. It is a challenge the youthful seeker cannot accept and he disappears from the pages of the gospels without a trace. He wanted to experience eternal life, but he could not escape the hold of earthly wealth. He is possessed by his possessions. If the prosperous farmer was *spiritually blinded* by riches, then this man is *spiritually bound* by them. And they keep him from finding God, from following Jesus and from serving the poor.

When we have grasped the import of these two incidents, we can more readily understand what Jesus means in his words about the poor in the passage we know as the 'Beatitudes': 'Blessed are the poor in spirit, for theirs is the Kingdom of heaven' (Mt. 5:3).

In Luke's parallel account, the words are addressed simply to 'you who are poor', but the meaning is essentially the same. It is the poor who appreciate the fragility of life and the insecurity of their position; it is the poor who consequently understand their utter dependency on God. Their material poverty leads them to a realisation of their spiritual poverty. The wealthy farmer and the rich young ruler are just as spiritually poor – even more so because, in the case of the farmer, he doesn't even realise his true condition and, in the case of the young man, he realises the truth but is unable to release himself from the prison his possessions have built around him.

But we have still to fathom the real depths of this central paradox of gospel and grace – that at one and the same time we must work for the elimination of poverty and yet willingly embrace it. For that we must give attention to some words that Paul wrote to the Corinthian church. As we have already noted, he had spoken to them 'about the collection' for the needy in Jerusalem in his first letter. He returns to the subject at greater depth when he writes to them again, encouraging them to complete what they had begun and to continue in their giving. He sets before them the example of their fellow-believers in the Macedonian churches who 'gave as much as they were able and even beyond their ability'. Then, as he so often does, he roots his appeal, not in cold morality but in sound theology; they should give, not just because of the needs of the poor, but also because of the nature of God; their giving must be more than just making a contribution, it should be rooted in a proper understanding of the miracle of the incarnation: 'I am not commanding you, but I want to test the sincerity of your love by comparing it with the earnestness of others. For you know the grace of our Lord Jesus Christ, that though he was rich, yet for your sakes he became poor, so that you through his poverty might become rich' (2 Cor. 8:8–9).

The eternal Word of God, from whom the whole created universe derives its existence, the One before whom every knee shall bow, the One in whom all the fullness of God resides – he gave up all his status, all his heavenly glory, was born the illegitimate son of a peasant girl, became a penniless wandering rabbi with no home of his own and died the death of a criminal. All for us! All so that we, who are spiritually bankrupt and morally destitute, should become rich in the sight of God. And that must be our example in giving. To embrace poverty in this way is far from the cold asceticism and legalistic self-denial that sometimes masquerades as the true Christian lifestyle. This is an expression of love. This is the willingness to forswear position and possessions for something of infinitely greater worth. This is the kind of poverty that loves people and parties; that transforms dull weddings into riotous celebrations and turns tepid, tasteless water into sparkling wine; that raises the dead and ruins funerals; that prefers the company of laughing children and repentant sinners to that of the smug, self-righteous religious leaders who parade their own piety and despise those who fail to come up to their standards. This is the kind of poverty that shows itself in a life that is free from selfishness, obedient to God's will and open in love to every person it encounters. *It is the kind of poverty that paradoxically and ironically enriches everyone it touches.* It is the poverty of the Son of God, who gave up everything to become the Son of Man, so that the sons and daughters of men might become the children of the living God and heirs to all the riches of heaven.

It is the joyful, extravagant poverty that is celebrated in the great hymn of Philippians chapter two, a hymn that praises the generosity of Jesus Christ, promises his ultimate victory over all things and prompts us to make his willing self-sacrifice the pattern for our lives

> Your attitude should be the same as that of Christ
>   Jesus:
> Who, being in very nature God
> did not consider equality with God something to be
>   grasped,
> but made himself nothing,
> taking the very nature of a servant,
> being made in human likeness.
> And being found in appearance as a man,
> he humbled himself
> and became obedient to death – even death on a cross!
> Therefore, God exalted him to the highest place
> and gave him the name that is above every name,
> that at the name of Jesus every knee should bow,
> in heaven and on earth and under the earth,
> and every tongue confess that Jesus Christ is Lord,
> to the glory of God the Father (Phil. 2:5–11).

The willing poverty we are trying to describe includes, but is not limited to, material possessions and money. Embracing poverty as Jesus embraced it demands a willingness to give up all claims to status, to rights and to privileges in order to serve and enrich the lives of others. For some, it will mean a literal vow of poverty, a rejection of the very concept of ownership and a refusal of all possessions apart from the very basic necessities of life. For all of us, it will entail a thorough examination of our personal lifestyles. We may well need to prepare a searching inventory of our spending and our habits in the light of the needs of others who have so little. We will endeavour to come to a *clarity in our thinking* which will enable us to distinguish between our needs and our wants; we will aim for a *simplicity in our lifestyle*, learning, as it has been expressed, 'to live more simply in order that others can simply live'; we will seek to develop *a sympathy for the plight of those who are less fortunate*, refusing to cocoon ourselves in ignorance which is anything but blissful; we will commit to a *generosity of spirit* that will look for opportunities to give wherever there is need; and we will experience the ultimate irony, the *liberty of soul* that comes from finding our true selves, as we willingly give up everything for the call of the gospel and the sake of a needy world.

Perhaps no-one has practised this paradox in our generation more beautifully or more persuasively than Mother Teresa of Calcutta. Whenever she expressed her faith in words, it was always so basic that, at first glance, it seemed little more than a compilation of clichés and truisms. But when the simplicity of her words is placed alongside the authenticity of her life, they carry an authority that demands quiet and thoughtful re-reading. Consider these remarks on what she believed made the work of her order so effective:

If we can see Jesus in the appearance of the bread (of the Eucharist), we can see him in the broken bodies of the poor. That is why we need that oneness with Christ, why we need that deep faith in Christ. It is very beautiful. When we have that deepening of contact with Christ and can accept him fully, we can touch the broken bodies. We put it into practice straight away. You need the poor to touch him . . . When I seek something for myself at the cost of everything else, I deliberately choose sin . . . I have put an obstacle between me and God . . . That's why poverty is such a wonderful gift of God for all of us – there are fewer obstacles. Very often in a desire to get something, there's greed, there's jealousy, there's distraction. We cannot see God then. It is an obstacle. More than any other Congregation, we need poverty, real poverty. It gives us the detachment and the real freedom necessary to understand the very poor people with whom we work.[13]

That is a hard counsel to follow and I for one would want to acknowledge how far short I fall from the standard of costly discipleship set by Mother Teresa and others like her. But we need to hear her words and we need to be challenged by her example. In a Church that is too often comfortable and self-absorbed, where some teach counterfeit doctrines of 'health and wealth', where others congratulate themselves on their cosy relationships with power-brokers and wealthy entrepreneurs and where most of us compromise daily with the godless materialism of our affluent culture, her words serve as a stinging but healing antiseptic to the poison that erodes our souls and numbs our consciences. We ignore such counsel at our peril. If we fail to practise, however imperfectly, the paradox of working to eliminate poverty while willingly embracing it, we will fail to show the world the terrible beauty of grace and gospel. Instead they will see only the hideous obscenity of a Church and a people who walk in the procession of the powerful and who follow the way of the wealthy.

Eight

prophecy: challenging the culture

Danger

The installation of Oscar Arnulfo Romero as
Archbishop of San Salvador on 22 February 1977 did
not exactly send waves of excitement and anticipation
through the Church. The growing social and political
tensions in El Salvador were matched by increasing
theological stresses in the Catholic Church surrounding the issue of liberation theology and the question
of how and whether the Church should stand openly
on the side of the lower classes. Against such a back-
ground, Romero was viewed by many as a 'safe pair
of hands', an orthodox, bookish conservative who
would preserve the status quo and negotiate a safe
passage for the Church through the stormy waters
swirling all around it. But events were to conspire to
change Romero quickly and dramatically; within a
few short weeks of taking office, the compromise
choice of the bishops became the uncompromising
voice of the poor. The studious priest became the zeal-
ous prophet. What had brought about such a transformation?

Just three weeks after Romero became Archbishop, his close friend, the Jesuit priest Rutilio Grande, was murdered on the road from Aguilares to El Paisnal, along with two of his parishioners, a young boy and an elderly man. Grande was targeted because of his commitment to the poor. He had defended the peasants' right to organize farm co-operatives, telling the wealthy landowners that their dogs ate better food than the children whose fathers worked in their fields. When Romero drove to El Paisnal to view the body of the murdered priest and his two parishioners, the direction of his life and ministry was changed forever. The frightened peasants who filled the church were like sheep without a shepherd; they were the disenfranchised without a spokesman. *And that was the moment when the sixty-year-old priest heard the call to be a prophet.* From that point onwards, in a series of weekly broadcasts, he encouraged his flock, not with promises of easy victory, but with the assurance that evil would never overcome good and that the Church of Jesus Christ would survive, not through its structures and its programmes, but in its people. They must share the prophetic calling of their leader. 'If some day they take away the radio station from us,' he said on one occasion, 'if they don't let us speak, if they kill all the priests and the bishop too and you are left a people without priests, each one of you must become God's microphone, each one of you must become a prophet.'

The United States of America, fearing that communism was about to establish itself in Central America, funded the right-wing forces whose violence was aimed at the poor. By 1980, the USA had been sending the equivalent of $1.5 million in military aid *every day* for twelve years. In that time, over 75,000 Salvadorans had been killed, one million had fled the country to escape the violence and one million more were homeless – all this in a nation whose total population was only 5.5 million people! In February of that year Romero appealed to President Jimmy Carter to end this support, but his pleas were refused. So on Sunday 23 March, he used his weekly homily to address the soldiers directly. Begging for an end to the violence and repression and appealing to the military to cease killing their own countrymen, he sounded a clarion call for the dawn of a new day: 'Brothers, you are from the same people; you kill your fellow-peasant . . . No soldier is obliged to obey an order contrary to the law of God . . . In the name of God then, in the name of this suffering people, I ask you, I beg you, I command you in the name of God: stop the repression.'[14]

The cathedral rang with thunderous applause. But in the eyes of the military leaders the Archbishop had gone too far: in effect, he had appealed for mutiny. The following day he was assassinated by one of the death squads who had wrought such havoc on his beloved country. But his life, his martyrdom and his ongoing influence in his own country and throughout the world are clear proof that speaking prophetically – being a voice for God in a violent world and protesting against the prevailing culture – is a vitally necessary but highly dangerous business.

Diminished

In recent decades, there has been an increased interest in the prophetic ministry in our churches and in so many ways this has been positive. We have discovered again that God can and does speak to and through his people. We have learned that, while the revelation of Scripture remains the standard against which everything must be tested, God can and does have a specific word for a particular situation at a particular time and place. We have recognised that there are those among us who are blessed with the capacity to hear from God and with the gift of passing on his message to the Church. And we have begun to appreciate that the five-fold ministry outlined in Ephesians – 'some to be apostles, some to be prophets, some to be evangelists and some to be pastors and teachers . . .' (Eph. 4:11) – is as relevant to the Church in the twenty-first century as it was in the first. All of this helps make for a healthy and functioning Church. But I sense that there is an increasing uneasiness about the ways in which prophecy is sometimes exercised and that we are in danger of being left with a impoverished version of this vital ministry. Let me suggest a number of examples of this diminished prophecy that we encounter in the Church today.

Perhaps the most common is *mini-prophecy* which reduces the mighty ministry of the prophetic to a series of kind and encouraging platitudes cast in the form of pleasing pastoral pictures. I hesitate to make the criticism because I recognise that it may look as if I am denigrating the ministry of good and sincere people. But I suspect I am not alone in being occasionally tempted to scream whenever someone approaches me to let me know that they have been given yet another picture of a river or mountains or whatever. They then usually follow this by giving me a brief – sometimes not so brief! – interpretation, or by asking me if I know what it means. I appreciate the concern they are showing and there are times when their words are genuinely helpful. My unease arises simply because it falls short of what I read of the exercise of the prophetic gift in Scripture.

Then there is the much more dangerous *manipulative-prophecy*. This occurs when someone takes it upon themselves to speak into the lives of others, giving direction on personal decisions as important as marriage, ministry, moving house, or changing church. A great deal of damage has been done to the lives of individuals and to the well-being of entire congregations. This is not to deny that there are occasions when people really do hear from God and are given the responsibility of sharing that word. But when that happens, there are safeguards that should always be put in place. The person sharing the prophetic word should test it with the leadership of the fellowship or with wise and mature Christians; and the individual or group to whom the prophecy is given should be strongly encouraged to test it by prayer, reflection, discussion with others and by asking if what they are being told is in line with the plain teaching of the Bible.

Some years ago, I attended a national conference at which we were told that one of the guest speakers, internationally known for his prophetic gifting, would minister in the final session of the day. I have never forgotten it. For about an hour he delivered personal prophecies to a number of high-profile leaders who were present, while the rest of us – several thousand people – listened in, looked on and felt left out. The sense that I had, which has only increased with the passage of time, was that I was witnessing *magic-prophecy*. The whole thing felt exactly like one of those television shows in which the fortune-teller or the medium amazes the audience by revealing details that they could not have known by normal rational means. I do not know where or how that man is ministering today and I would be very reluctant to attribute his knowledge to sources other than the Holy Spirit. But I do know that there was no sense of God being glorified or the Church of Jesus Christ been built up in its faith and fellowship. At the very least, it remains a warning that too great an emphasis on skilful presentation or personal gifting can result in ministry degenerating into glossy performance.

Since that time, there has been a greater emphasis on prophecy as the delivery of God's word to challenge the prevailing culture and this surely represents the recovery of a vital aspect of the prophetic calling. But all too often what we see and hear is a kind of *mad-at-everybody-prophecy*. Recently I received an email from someone who had heard me speaking on national radio and wanted to quote me in his forthcoming book. Like most other speakers, I'm vulnerable to a little flattery and I'm always pleased when someone wants to quote me as an authority. On this occasion, however, it was not difficult to resist the approach. The proposed title of his book indicated clearly that the writer believed the entire nation is under the sway of Satan and, as far as I could judge, the contents were devoted to a passionate denunciation of just about everyone and everything in Britain today. The trouble with this kind of prophetic 'carpet bombing' is that all it succeeds in doing is convincing non-believers that Christians are unsympathetic and angry people whose primary task in life is to find out how and why others are enjoying themselves and put a stop to it. And when it is specific, it usually concentrates on personal sins, particularly those of a sexual nature and says nothing about corporate and structural sins which keep so many of our fellow human beings in poverty and oppression.

Direction

Despite the diminished versions of prophecy that we have identified, however, the prophetic voice remains essential to the well-being of the Church itself and to the role of the Church in the wider society. It represents one vitally important means by which God chooses to address us in the contemporary situation. This is certainly an area where the correct response to misuse and abuse is not non-use but the *right* use. We need to find a direction for this ministry that will allow us to exercise it in ways that will challenge both the Church and the culture in which we are called to be faithful witnesses to gospel truth. A brief survey of prophecy in the Bible will provide us with some helpful signs that will point us in the right direction.

The Old Testament prophets: rooted in God's will

One of the most remarkable features of the Old Testament, of the religion of the Jewish people and of their encounter with God, is the line of prophets which extends from the time of Samuel, eleven centuries before the coming of Christ, right through to the ministry of Malachi some seven hundred years later. They prophesy in different times and in widely differing situations, but the impetus for their ministry comes always from the same source: God has rescued Israel from slavery, chosen them as his people and called them to reflect his holiness to the nations around him by obeying his laws. Yet time after time, with a predictability that is both wearisome and frustrating, Israel is unfaithful to the covenant God has made with them. The task of the prophets – the very reason for their existence – is to remind them of that covenant and to call them back to God's will for them as his people. And that prophetic call is sounded without fear or favour to the people in general and to the rich and powerful in particular, both in the political and religious realms. The prophets announce God's judgement on his people, but it is always judgement with a purpose, discipline that carries a hope for the future. When God punishes them, it may feel as if he has stopped loving them, but the opposite is the case; because he has chosen them, because he loves them, he will never give up on them and he disciplines them only to bring them to their senses and back to his purposes for them. Amos sums up the essence of the prophetic message in a few short sentences

> I brought you up out of Egypt,
> and I led you for forty years in the desert
> to give you the land of the Amorites.
> I also raised up prophets from among your sons . . .
> Hear this word the Lord has spoken against you, O
>   people of Israel . . .
> You only have I chosen
> of all the families of the earth;
> therefore I will punish you
> for all your sins (Amos 2:10,11; 3:1,2).

Each of the prophets brings his own emphasis, depending on the situation in which he is called to minister, but always it is a variation on the same theme: Israel has been chosen to be the people of God and the standard to which she is called is governed neither by the status quo nor by what is acceptable to other nations; *her calling is to do God's will*. For Elijah, for example, that means standing against the idolatry that threatens Israel's very identity and insisting that Yahweh alone is to be worshipped; for Amos, it means demanding the people act with justice and fairness, particularly to the poor and needy, because the God of Israel is a righteous God; for Isaiah, it means holding in tension the majestic holiness and merciful forgiveness of God; for Jeremiah, it means painting a picture of a God who not only judges and disciplines his people, but who also shares their sufferings; for Ezekiel, it means pointing to the restoration and return to their homeland that would follow the rebuke of exile.

In each of those various situations the prophet's message is a combination of *forth-telling* – announcing God's word for that time and place – and *fore-telling* – pointing to what God will do, a future that is conditional on the response of the hearers to the call that has been sounded to repent and do God's will. And through it all, as they discern and declare the word and will of God, they increasingly look forward to a great climax to Israel's history, the 'day of the Lord' and the coming of the Messiah, God's Anointed One, a time when the things that were partially fulfilled would come to perfect fruition.

John the Baptist: repentance and guilt

The Old Testament prophets were not to see that come to pass in their lifetimes. In fact, for four centuries following the time of Malachi, the prophetic voice was silent in Israel until the coming of John the Baptist. When the gospel writers tell us that John came preaching in the desert and that his 'clothes were made of camel's hair, with a leather belt around his waist' (Mt. 1:6), they are doing more than simply pointing out the location of his ministry and describing his apparel. They are inviting the reader to understand what John's original audience would have recognised immediately: this is a man whose whole way of life and appearance is unmistakably reminiscent of the prophets of old. And the tone and content of his message confirm that this is the authentic voice of the prophet. Even the Pharisees and

Sadducees who make the journey to the desert to hear him are not allowed to take refuge in their status as 'the chosen people'; instead, they are confronted with their guilt and called to repentance

> You brood of vipers! Who warned you to flee from the coming wrath? Produce fruit in keeping with repentance. And do not think you can say to yourselves, 'We have Abraham as our father.' I tell you that out of these stones God can raise up children for Abraham. The axe is already at the root of the trees and every tree that does not produce good fruit will be cut down and thrown into the fire (Mt. 3:7–10).

But for all his fiery rhetoric and fierce censure, there is a recognition in John's heart and mind that the content of his message is limited and that its context is to prepare his hearers for something better. The best he can do is to get people ready for something far greater, for *Someone* whose ministry will reach far deeper than his own. 'I baptise you with water for repentance. But after me will come one who is more powerful than I, whose sandals I am not fit to carry. He will baptise you with the Holy Spirit and with fire . . .' (Mt. 3:11).

Jesus: renewal and grace

The One who is to come is, of course, Jesus himself – the One in whom the message and ministry of the prophets will be brought to completion. It is not simply the *predictions* of the ancient prophets that are fulfilled in Jesus, though that is true to a quite remarkable extent, particularly in his suffering, death and resurrection; equally important is the fact that all the things that they *proclaimed* – the majesty of God, his covenant with his people, the obedience he demands from them, the discipline he imposes on them, his refusal ever to forsake them – are embodied and brought to perfection in the perfect and complete ministry of Jesus. If the prophetic calling is to declare the word of God to his people, then Jesus – the Word made flesh – is the greatest of all the prophets.

He himself made that clear in his 'parable of the tenants' (Mk. 12:1–11), a barbed tale of a landowner who sends a series of messengers to his vineyard to collect the rent due to him. One after another, they are beaten up and killed by the defiant tenants. In the end, the master sends his own son whom he loves dearly, but he, too, is murdered. The import of the story was not lost on the religious leaders of his day. They knew all too clearly that the messengers were the prophets of Israel and that Jesus was claiming both to stand in the line of the prophets and to be in a unique relationship to his Father God.

What distinguishes the ministry of Jesus from all that has gone before is that while, like the prophets, he sees the will of God as the bottom line on everything and while, like John the Baptist, he knows all too well the guilt of his hearers and calls for their repentance, *he has come to give himself for them*. In his life, in his atoning death and in his resurrection he will offer *grace* and *renewal* – the unmerited forgiveness of God and the unlimited power of the Holy Spirit. The prophetic message that demands complete obedience to the will of God has become flesh in the perfect man who gives that complete obedience on our behalf. The call of the prophet and the response of the willing seeker after God have been brought together in the person of Jesus. The prophetic ministry will never be the same again.

The Early Church: revelation and growth

Even a cursory read through the book of Acts and the New Testament letters will leave no room for doubt that the ministry of the prophet was extensively exercised and highly valued in the Early Church. We are told, for example, that Agabus is part of a group of prophets who travel from the church in Jerusalem to Antioch, where they predict a widespread famine which provokes the believers into taking up an offering to provide help for their fellow-Christians in Judea (Acts 11:27–30). A little later, Judas and Silas, 'who themselves were prophets' (Acts 15:32), make the same journey 'to encourage and strengthen the brothers' in the light of the instructions that have been issued by the apostles regarding the admission of Gentiles to the church. And later still, Agabus appears again, this time warning Paul that imprisonment awaits him in Jerusalem (Acts 21:10). There can be no doubt that the God-given insights and Spirit-filled encouragement of the prophets were a significant factor of life in the Church.

Just why they had such a valued ministry can be seen from Paul's advice to the church in Corinth about the use of spiritual gifts. In one very illuminating passage, he contrasts prophecy with the gift of tongues and explains why he regards prophecy so highly and why he would encourage all God's people to seek and to exercise this gift

> Follow the way of love and eagerly desire spiritual gifts, especially the gift of prophecy. For anyone who speaks in a tongue does not speak to men but to God. Indeed, no-one understands him; he utters mysteries with his spirit. But everyone who prophesies speaks to men for their strengthening, encouragement and comfort. He

who speaks in a tongue edifies himself, but he who prophesies edifies the church . . . So if the whole church comes together and everyone speaks in tongues and some who do not understand or some unbelievers come in, will they not say that you are out of your mind? But if an unbeliever or someone who does not understand comes in while everybody is prophesying, he will be convinced by all that he is a sinner and will be judged by all and the secrets of his heart will be laid bare. So he will fall down and worship God, exclaiming, 'God is really among you!' (1 Cor. 14:1–4,23–25).

Clearly, Paul regards prophecy so highly because, firstly, it *reveals God's message* for his people in their particular situation and secondly, because it leads to the *growth of the Church*, not only by 'edifying' those who were already followers of Jesus, but also by convicting those who witnessed the life and worship of the Church and who heard God's word in language that they understood.

Prophecy today: learning the lessons

When we reflect on this brief survey of prophecy in the Bible – the Old Testament prophets, John the Baptist, Jesus himself and the Early Church – there are lessons that begin to emerge for us today from each of these men and movements. Our starting point, like the ancient prophets of Israel, must be *the word and the will of God*. We speak to the great moral and spiritual issues of the world in which we live, not in a desperate attempt to make the Church or the gospel *relevant*, or even because we want to make sure that the Christian voice is heard in the world, but because our God – the God of the Bible – has revealed himself as a *righteous* God. We stand against oppression, injustice, immorality and dishonesty because they offend our God, who calls the human race into a covenant relationship with him.

The prophetic stance of the Church is not an 'add-on' to our worship or an 'optional extra' to the work of evangelism. It is intrinsic to our mission as the Church in the world. Equally, like John the Baptist, we will not shy away from addressing the issue of human guilt – both personal and corporate – for the hurts and pain of the world. We will not shy away from challenging individuals, communities, nations and governments to face the reality of sin. We will not yield to those who try to silence us by telling us that 'religion is a private matter'; on the contrary, we will insist that, while faith is personal, it also has a *public* dimension and that the kingdoms of this world are also the kingdoms of our God. And we will call fearlessly and without apology for repentance, both individual and corporate, wherever God's laws of personal integrity and social justice have been broken.

But, if we are to be true to Scripture, we will not stop – as too often, I fear, has been the case – at the prophetic lessons of the Old Testament and of John the Baptist. We will always remember that the greatest of the prophets is Jesus himself, in whom the declaration of truth and righteousness are always perfectly matched by the offer of *grace* and the promise of *renewal*. In him, the wrath of a holy God is perfectly balanced by the compassion of a loving Father: it is a perfect balance that he reveals not only in his condemnation of sin, but also in his costly self-sacrifice for a lost world. Too often, when Christians speak out on moral issues, the impression we give to non-believers is simply that we are angry, unhappy and unsympathetic people.

That is particularly the case when we face issues of personal sexual morality. Indeed, our critics would say that sometimes we seem to be obsessed by other people's sexual sins to the exclusion of everything else. I am sure that I am not the only person to notice that Jesus, on the other hand, always approached people who were overtaken in sexual sin with an understanding and sympathy that restored rather than robbed them of their dignity. When he met the Samaritan woman by the well in the midday heat, he gave her back her dignity by asking her for a drink and engaging her in a conversation that recognised her as a person of worth. When he was confronted with the woman taken in adultery, he refused to condemn her but sent her on her way, encouraging her to leave her sinful past behind. It seems that Jesus instinctively realised that sexual sin is often an expression of a low self-esteem. We must follow him in giving as much attention to restoring the personal dignity of sinners as we do to challenging their personal moral lapses.

And, if we take into account the total picture of prophecy in the Bible, we will recognise that in the New Testament Church, the *revelation* of God's word and the *growth* of his Church were such significant factors precisely because of what we might call the *democratisation* of prophecy. It is Paul's expressed wish for the Corinthians that all of God's people should prophesy and, in stating that desire, he is in tune with Peter's description of the work of the Spirit on the day of Pentecost: 'I will pour out my Spirit *on all people* . . . and they will prophesy (Acts 2:17,18). Of course, as with every other spiritual gift, there will be some who will exercise this particular ministry to a greater extent than the majority of us. But we will not be true to the New Testament if we fail to take seriously the fact that prophecy is the task of the whole Church. We must all listen to the voice of God, we must all speak his word as he enables us. To put it another way, the Church must become a *prophetic community*. And that surely means more than just 'speaking out' the truth; we must also *live it out*. Actions, it is rightly said, speak louder than words. The world will not heed either our proclamation of the gospel or our protests against evil, unless that proclamation and protest come from a community that demonstrates by its corporate life the truth it seeks to declare.

That will mean putting out own house in order before we try to set the world to rights. We cannot protest against exploitation of the poor if we spend more on the maintenance of our buildings than on the care of the needy; we cannot protest against a lack of sexual discipline in our society if we ourselves are guilty of uncontrolled gluttony and gossip; we cannot plead for an end to war if churches cannot get over their minor difficulties and work together to bless our communities; we cannot challenge our political masters about their conduct if Christian leaders create structures of church government that allow them to become unaccountable for their actions. The prophetic ministry will call us to a radical examination of the true condition of the Church as much as to a risky declaration of the truth to society.

Delivery

If we were to ask any group of people to describe their experience of the prophetic ministry in just one or two words, a few at least, I suspect, might use the word 'terrible'. Some might use that word as it is normally used in colloquial English – meaning 'really bad' – if they have encountered someone who has abused this ministry. Others, who have encountered something of the power of prophecy, might use the word in its more technically correct sense of 'provoking terror or awe'. But I'm not sure if anyone would use the word 'beautiful' about prophecy. And that, it seems to me, is a great pity, because it indicates that there are two things about this ministry that we have forgotten and consequently neglected in the manner in which we exercise it today. If we could rediscover and reclaim them, we might once again witness the *terrible beauty* of the prophetic when it touches seemingly hard hearts and transforms apparently hopeless situations.

The power of words

Firstly, we have forgotten that when the ancient prophets delivered their message, it was not simply a powerful overflowing of human emotion or even of divine energy, although those two characteristics were most definitely present. We have failed to notice the fact that the prophets crafted their message carefully and honed their words to perfection in order to arrest the attention of their hearers and to lodge the message deep in their imaginations as well as in their minds. The Old Testament prophetic writings are much closer to poetry than to cold prose. They are full of imaginative figures of speech and powerful dramatic images – everything from baskets of fruit to bears that devour the unwary. They employ the technique of Hebrew poetry, which works not by rhyming but by parallel couplets, which state the same thing in two different ways to reinforce the message. To take one example at random from the prophecy of Amos

> Does a lion roar in the thicket
> when he has no prey?

> Does he growl in his den
> When he has caught nothing?
>
> (Amos 3:4)

Sometimes the prophets will construct entire passages where the rhythm builds until the climax of the message comes with a force that would have shocked the original hearers. (We need to appreciate the fact that these words would have been recited in the market-place rather read in the library!) Again Amos provides a wonderful example of this. His prophecy begins with a long tirade against Israel's neighbours. The language and the rhythm are hypnotic

> This is what the Lord says:
> For three sins of Damascus,
> even for four, I will not turn back my wrath . . .
>
> (Amos 1:3).

For verse after verse, he continues with the same pattern of words, moving from Damascus to Gaza, to Tyre, to Edom, to Ammon and to Moab, outlining both their sins and the punishment that is about to fall on them. By the time he reaches Moab, the rhythm of the verse would have had the assembled crowd in a state of high excitement and they might well be literally cheering and applauding; for these are all Israel's enemies and they deserve everything that is coming to them. Then, when their defences are down, the prophet goes for the jugular!

> This is what the Lord says:
> For three sins of Judah,
> even for four, I will not turn back my wrath.
> Because they have rejected the law of the Lord . . .

I will send fire upon Judah
that will consume the fortresses of Jerusalem
(Amos 2:4,5).

This is not what they are expecting. *God is judging the people of Israel as well as the surrounding nations!* The impact is great, because the prophet has reflected on the word from God, exercised his poetic gifting and constructed his language in such a skilful, powerful manner that his message has maximum effect.

The power of action

The second thing we have neglected to notice is that the prophets were not limited to words. They also appreciated and utilised the power of symbol and drama to communicate their messages. Jeremiah, for example, was prophesying in the second half of the sixth century BC, just prior to Jerusalem being over-run by its enemies. But shortly before the fall of the city he did something that must have seemed very odd to his contemporaries. He purchased a field from his cousin Hanamel, a field which was situated three miles outside of the city in land already occupied by the enemy! Jeremiah's business transaction must have been a topic of conversation and he would have been the butt of many a joke – until his critics reflected on what he had done. For this was a symbolic action, announcing, far more powerfully than words ever could, that the land belonged to God and would one day be restored to his people. Somewhat different but just as dramatic was Isaiah's action in walking around barefoot and naked for three years as a prophetic warning to those who favoured alliances with Egypt (Isa. 20:1–6). The power of the Egyptians is illusory, Isaiah was saying; before long they will be led captive and naked by the king of Assyria. Such examples of dramatic symbolism can be multiplied many times in the prophets of the Old Testament.

Now I am neither recommending nudity nor even a return to Hebrew poetry as useful prophetic tools in the twenty-first century! But there are serious points to be made about the way in which we deliver the prophetic message. Just like the prophets of old, we too must hone our communication skills if we are to deliver effectively what we believe God wants us to say to an audience that may not want to hear it. There are few things more dispiriting than to witness a Christian taking part in a discussion programme on radio or TV, using words and phrases that are not understood outside of Christian circles, or making it evident that they are locked into thought forms that are no longer part of the mental currency of the age in which we live. The content of the message will only be heard and understood by a secular audience if we are wise enough and work hard enough to learn and apply the methods of communication that are appropriate to that audience.

In addition, the prophets have much to teach us in their use of symbol and drama in communicating their message. I have a suspicion that in order to reach our generation with God's word for today, we will need to place greater value on and make far more effective use of the arts. The cinema, radio and television, the theatre, the novel and the concert hall are – far more than we realise – the places where the big questions are being asked, where most people reflect on the big issues of our day and where many, without fully realising it, find their answers and imbibe their values. The church needs to nurture and release its painters, poets, musicians, dancers and actors – all those skilled in the arts. We need to find ways of helping them immerse their thinking and creativity in the will and the word of God, so that what they express in their art is, above everything else, a prophetic word to their audiences. That is not to say that everything they do should be evangelistic or even that it need be overtly 'Christian art'. It does mean that all their work should be marked by excellence, since their talents are first and foremost a gift from God and an offering to God. And it does mean that all they do will be under-pinned by the life-values and worldview that come from knowing God, sharing in his creativity and believing that all men and women are created in his image and loved by him.

A Church that values and affirms its artists will increasingly discover that its own life and worship as the people of God will be enhanced as we apprehend God with our imaginations as well as our intellects. When we allow God to engage with our humanity in its totality – spiritually, emotionally, imaginatively and physically – we will find that our personal spirituality, our efforts to evangelise others and even the physical environment in which we conduct our worship will all be marked by an excellence that would otherwise be beyond our experience. Such a community of believers will also be increasingly effective in the prophetic min-istry. That is not to suggest that we will find easy answers to difficult questions for ourselves or that we will provide such easy answers for others. The grace of God, as we have sought to emphasise throughout this book, is as uncompromising and uncomfortable in its perfecting of us as it is unconditional in its accepting of us. And the calling of a prophetic community will be no more and no less than to communicate that terrible beauty of unconquerable love and uncompromising grace to a world that needs to be wooed as much as it needs to be transformed.

Nine

preaching: addressing the Church

For a number of years I've been a regular contributor as the 'faith guest' on Radio Two's *Good Morning Sunday* programme. For most of that time, they've introduced me on air by referring to my title as a denominational leader in the north west of England. The first time I took part in the show after I had relinquished that position, they couldn't make up their minds as to how they should introduce me in a way that would make it clear to the listening audience that my ministry now is essentially one of speaking and writing. Even though I suggested that I'd be more than happy if they just said my name, they were adamant that I needed some kind of title or descriptive label. Which is why, as I was driving into the studio, I heard the presenter announce, 'Our guest in the studio today will be the preacher, Chick Yuill.' The odd thing was that, despite the fact that I've always regarded preaching as my primary calling and one of the main reasons that God allows me to take up space on the earth, it sounded very strange and somewhat old-fashioned. It made me feel a bit like a character in one of those old Westerns; you know the kind of thing I mean: 'The preacher's a good man and he's riding into town, but he

won't fire a gun even if those bandits attack his family!'
And I realised that, though I've been introduced as 'the
preacher' on a Sunday morning in church just to let
everybody know why I was there, nobody had ever used
the word to describe who I *am* and what I *do*.

Maybe I was just surprised that someone was recognising that preaching is a legitimate and even a significant way in which to spend your life and expend your
energies. That certainly isn't always the case. Wikipedia,
the web-based encyclopaedia whose content is written
by volunteers from all over the world, may not be the
last word in accuracy or erudition; but when it offers its
definition of preaching, it undoubtedly expresses what a
great many people think. Here is the gist of its opening
paragraph on the subject: 'Sermons are usually, but not
always, delivered in a house of worship, most of which
have a pulpit . . . In modern language, the word "sermon" can also be used pejoratively in secular terms to
describe a lengthy or tedious speech delivered with
great passion, by any person, to an uninterested audience.'

If only we could dismiss those words as being the
misguided opinion of those outside the Church who
have nothing more than a secondhand and distorted
notion of what preaching really is. Alas, I suspect that
many who attend places of Christian worship Sunday
by Sunday would have some sympathy with these sen-
timents. More times than I want to admit I have been in
church when it was announced that, for some reason or
other, next week's service would not feature a sermon
and on almost all those occasions the announcement has
been greeted by a cheer.

Something has clearly gone wrong; it was never
meant to be like this. Contrast the cynical comments of
Wikipedia with the book of Acts. On the Day of

Pentecost, the descent of the Holy Spirit on the believers meant that Peter had to deliver the first sermon in the history of the Church to explain what had happened and why. The impact was immediate and enormous – three thousand people became believers in response to the preaching of the good news about Jesus. This was anything but 'a lengthy or tedious speech delivered with great passion to an uninterested audience'. The powerful dynamic of New Testament preaching is highlighted by the three Greek words that are characteristically used to describe this activity: *evangelizesthai* meaning 'to deliver good news', *katangellein* meaning 'to declare or announce' and *kerussein* meaning 'to proclaim as a herald would do'. This kind of preaching demanded a decision and was guaranteed to provoke a reaction – either open-hearted acceptance or out and out antagonism – but it was definitely never boring or tedious.

Of course, it can be and often is argued that preaching in the New Testament is not exactly the same as what we call preaching today. The former is all about bringing good news to those who don't yet know Jesus; the latter is more to do with teaching believers, an activity for which the New Testament employs the word *didache* meaning 'instructions regarding correct belief and right behaviour'. That is a valid distinction, but it is one that I am convinced has been pressed too hard.

We, too, are called upon to announce the good news of the gospel and to deliver evangelistic messages to unbelievers. And the people in our church pews may not be as different from the crowd who had gathered in Jerusalem on the Day of Pentecost as we imagine. More than a few who attend our churches are like those 'God-fearing Jews' (Acts 2:5) who heard Peter preach; they, too, have a knowledge of God and a concern to worship him that brings them to our churches and to our religious festivals,

but they are often lacking first-hand experience of the difference that the presence and power of the risen, living
Jesus can make in their lives through the Holy Spirit. For
their sakes – and for the sake of any who hear us – our
preaching must have that same terrible beauty that cuts to
the heart and leaves men and women asking not, 'When
does the service finish?' but 'What shall we do?' (Acts
2:37)

In order to draw that response from them, the question we must face is, 'What do we – both preacher and
congregation – need to do so that the authentic, terrible
but beautiful, voice of God is heard through us and
among us?' I offer humbly, but with all the conviction I
can muster, a four-fold answer to that all-important
enquiry. My comments are not about the technique of
preaching – such things as the construction and delivery
of a sermon – though there certainly is a place for such
guidance. But those are matters for a very different kind
of book from this. My concerns relate to the spiritual
heart of the matter and the very purpose of this crucial
and vital aspect of the Church's calling.

Entering the sanctuary – prayerfully and corporately

Preaching is not the same as delivering a lecture on theology or on some biblical topic. A lecture is a work of
scholarship and its chief purpose is the education of
those who attend the lecture; they should know more –
or at least be in a better position to ask the right questions – at the end of the lecture than they did at the
beginning. And that's a laudable purpose. We need to be
educated and informed in order that we can think
Christianly in a world that is often ignorant about

Christian values and apathetic or even antagonistic towards the truth of Scripture. But preaching is essentially different, even though it may, indeed must, contain some of the elements of a lecture, such as sound biblical interpretation, reasoned theological reflection and intelligent and relevant application of truth. Preaching is not primarily about the *education* of people; it is much more about their *transformation*. Whereas the lecture is prepared in the *study*, preaching is brought to birth in the *sanctuary*. A good lecture is forged when a man or woman spends time reading, thinking and reflecting; a genuine sermon is birthed only when a man or a woman spends time praying, meditating and listening to God.

It was Phillips Brooks who famously and perceptively described preaching as 'truth mediated through personality'. That being the case, it is not difficult to understand that preaching is meaningful and effective only when those who have that responsibility open themselves up to God, allowing Jesus, *the living word*, to speak to their hearts through the Bible, *the written Word*, in order that those who receive what is preached may hear the authentic voice of God in and through *the spoken word* of the preacher. This is not to deny that, as with all human activity, some will be more gifted in preaching than others, and that natural talents and God-given gifts – or, in some cases, the lack of them – of the preacher will have an impact positively or negatively in the communication of the truth. But it is to insist that, without the encounter with God in the sanctuary of his presence, true preaching, preaching that reaches both head and heart, will never take place.

It is not just the preacher, however, who needs to be alone with God. If the preacher is responsible for sowing the seed of God's word, the congregation is largely accountable for tilling and preparing the soil. Preaching is never so powerful as when it is received by a company of people in an atmosphere that is soaked in prayer and charged with an expectancy that God will speak. The most nervous and inexperienced preachers have found themselves mightily used by God in such situations. The undue adulation of popular and gifted speakers and the cult of 'sermon-tasting' should have no place among us. Prayer and encouragement for whoever has the responsibility for opening the word should be the order of the day. We don't meet to be entertained or, dare I say it, even to 'be blessed'. We come together to be challenged by the word of unconditional love and uncompromising authority.

The fact that preaching is an interplay between the preacher, the people of God and the power of God opens the door to all kinds of exciting possibilities and raises all kinds of challenging questions. Does the fact that traditionally we have seen the sermon as being delivered by one person – most often a male – to a group of more or less passive listeners mean that this is the only way it should happen? Is there room for a greater level of democracy and a stronger element of discovery in preaching? In a visual, multi-media age, is the spoken word still the best or the only way to declare timeless truth? How can the use of drama or movie clips enhance our encounter with God's word? How much space should be given to discussion and debate, or to periods of silent contemplation to allow us to reflect on what God is saying? Who should set the agenda for the Bible passages and topics that are taught throughout the year – the preacher, a preaching team, or the congregation?

An exploration of these questions is beyond the scope of this book, but we can and must say this: it is time for us to move beyond the mind-set that sees the preacher as source of all authority and the congregation merely as those who turn up to be told what to believe. That kind of thinking is unfair to the preacher because it places far too great a responsibility on them for the spiritual well-being of the rest of us. It can also lead to too much stress on the authority of one individual, with all the consequences of such an overemphasis. In addition, it is unhelpful to the Body of Christ in any local church, in that it allows us to lapse into the attitude whereby we neglect our personal daily spiritual discipline and expect the preacher to do for us on Sundays what we should be doing throughout the week. In short, we need to see the preacher not as the fount of all knowledge, but as the one who has been allowed to spend a little more time at the well filling the jars with the water of life. And when that water is shared in the presence of Jesus, the living Word, it is wonderfully and miraculously transformed into a sparkling wine, a heady brew of refreshing and stimulating divine truth that sets our hearts racing and our feet dancing to the rhythm of the life of the Spirit.

Telling the story – completely and relevantly

Recently I attended a very stimulating meeting of some local church leaders with representatives of the Bible Society. We had deliberately chosen a room right at the top of one Manchester's hotels. The room, which provides a panoramic view of much of the city, is appropriately called 'The Sky Lounge' and it provided a fitting venue for a conversation that centred on the challenge of making the Bible accessible and credible to our fellow-citizens. During the course of the meeting, someone from the Bible Society made one of those statements that really shakes you because it contains a truth that you've failed to notice properly, despite the fact that it's been

staring you in the face for years. What she said was this:
'The Bible is 80 per cent narrative, but we confine most
of our preaching to the remaining 20 per cent – the New
Testament Letters, the Psalms and the wisdom literature.' No one would want to deny that these parts of the
Bible are important and that they contain doctrinal and
ethical teaching that is relevant to the Church in every
age and in every culture. But our comparative neglect of
the major proportion of Scripture is troubling and indicates a major weakness in our preaching.

I suggest that one of the reasons people often find
preaching boring and irrelevant is that what we give
them – a theology to reflect upon or a philosophy to live
by – is not what they are *primarily* looking for. Nor,
indeed, is it what the Bible is *primarily* concerned with.
They are not even looking primarily for answers to questions. (Even when we come up with answers, they're
often not related to the questions people are asking in
any case!) They are looking for a story that makes some
kind of sense of life in all its awesome wonder and con-
fusing complexity, something that ties it all together,
something that has a beginning and an end, a theme and
a purpose. It is time to tell the *whole* story in our preaching, the great sweep of the Bible from the creation of the
universe to the consummation of all things in the coming of Christ, including the twists and turns of God's
dealings with his people Israel and all the sub-plots with
their little stories of individuals, some of whom served
God well, all of whom served him imperfectly.

In a beautifully written passage, the German theologian, Helmut Thielicke, describes the powerful
preaching of one of his heroes and one of the greatest
preachers of the nineteenth century, C.H. Spurgeon.
Thielicke is filled with admiration, not for his subject's
erudition as a theologian or for his skill in the exegesis of

difficult doctrinal passages, but simply for his ability to make the characters and events of the Bible vivid and real from the pulpit.

> When (Charles Haddon) Spurgeon speaks, it is as if the figures of the patriarchs and prophets and apostles were in the auditorium – sitting upon a raised tribune! – looking down upon the listeners. You hear the rush of the Jordan and the murmuring of the brooks of Siloam; you see the cedars of Lebanon swaying in the wind, hear the clash and tumult of battle between the children of Israel and the Philistines, sense the safety and security of Noah's ark, suffer the agonies of soul endured by Job and Jeremiah, hear the creak of oars as the disciples strain against the contrary winds, and feel the dread of the terrors of the apocalypse. The Bible is so close that you not only hear its messages, but breathe its very atmosphere. The heart is so full of Scripture that it leavens the consciousness, peoples the imagination with its images and determines the landscape of the soul by its climate. And because it has what might be called a total presence, the Bible as the Word of God is really concentrated life that enters every pore and teaches us not only to see and hear but also to taste and smell the wealth of reality that is spread out before us here.[15]

We need to learn to preach like that for our generation. Of course, our language and our style will be very different from that of Spurgeon, but our aim will be the same – to make the Bible live in all its vivid colours and in all its complex tapestry of people and events. That will mean telling the stories of Jesus and his encounters with a variety of people and telling them in ways that draw our hearers into the narrative, so that they themselves can stand there in the presence of the Master, hear him speak to them and feel his healing touch. It will mean giving more time to telling the story of the cross than to attempting to explain it and telling it with such passion and power that the hearts of men and women are broken by the sights and sounds of Calvary.

It will mean telling the stories of the Old Testament with a God-given imagination that enables us to take others with us as we enter into a world and a way of thinking that is often very different from ours. It will mean telling the difficult parts of the story, witnessing the bloody battles with Israel's enemies and going to the places where God seems stern and angry and very different from what we want him to be, but acknowledging that it is all part of the awesome nature of a God who is bigger than our puny minds.

It will mean that sometimes we have to confess that, just as we don't always understand fully what wiser people have to say to us, so sometimes we don't understand perfectly the word of God in this or that passage of Scripture. But through it all, we will confess our faith: we know the Divine Author of Scripture, we have seen his face in Jesus, we have experienced the touch of his Spirit through his word, through his good creation and through his Body, the church. And we are willing and determined to listen to him even when his message is too great and too rich to be fully clear to our finite minds.

Doing theology – boldly and lovingly

Such preaching means that we will seek to hold firmly to the essential truths that bind us together as followers of Jesus, truths on which there can be no wavering and no equivocation. We will preach that Jesus is God's unique and perfect revelation of himself to humanity, the One in whom all the fullness of the Father is pleased to dwell; we will preach that the Scriptures of the Old and New Testaments are given by the inspiration of the Holy Spirit and that they are the supreme authority in all matters of faith and conduct; we will preach that the death of Jesus at Calvary dealt with the consequences of human sin and that all who turn to Jesus and trust him are brought into a new relationship with God our Father; we will preach that, as children of God and in the power of the Holy Spirit, we must demonstrate that new relationship in changed lives that reflect the life of Jesus himself; we will preach that being in a new relationship with God brings us into a new relationship with our fellow believers as members of the Body of Christ in his Church; and we will preach that God's ultimate purpose is the renewal of the entire created order and that we must actively work to that end until God's great mission of redemption is complete at the coming of Christ. On those great truths, we will stand firm in our preaching and in our living.

In a post-modern world, where relativism is the order of the day and where tolerance rather than truth is regarded as the supreme virtue, we will not yield in our conviction that God has spoken in Jesus, the living Word, and through Scripture, the written word, and that his word is truth for all time and for every culture. But that is not to say that we will be afraid to re-think and re-phrase our theology; we need to do that precisely because our calling is to be true to God's word and not our own paraphrase of that word, however hallowed and honoured that paraphrase might be by time and tradition. Brian McLaren's courageous comments on this matter deserve to be quoted and pondered on again and again:

What a change occurs . . . when we see the theologian as the creative thinker, the pursuer of truth, the whole-hearted seeker, explorer and learner, rather than the memorizer, repeater and defender of old formulations. What a challenge we encounter when we open ourselves to discover how Jesus Christ wants to theologically incarnate himself in the post-modern world, just as he did for the post-enlightenment world of the old church . . .

. . . we will be aware that our message is not perfect. God's message is perfect; but all of our versions of it are always to some degree out of sync with his version. To the degree that we are trying to get our message straight, we have to admit that there is some need for changing it. This is a risky, dangerous enterprise with much at stake. For this reason, theology in the new church is more important, not less important, than in the old church, which felt that it already has the message straight and simply needed to proclaim it and defend it . . .

If, in the new paradigm of theology, we keep trusting that the Word beneath our words is there, if we lean on God and not on our own understanding (even our own understanding of God), if we can doubt ourselves and our cogitation while we trust in the living God who is with us, if our hearts are right – then maybe we can have creativity and truth-seeking without jailing so many Galileos, burning so many John Huses, damning so many Martin Luthers and Martin Luther Kings and thus pruning off the green growth at the ends of our branches.[16]

May God grant all of his Church the grace – but perhaps especially those of us who gladly and gratefully stand within the evangelical tradition – to heed those words as we seek to preach 'the old, old story of Jesus and his love' in ways and with words and that can be understood by our peers and to cast our theology in thought forms of post-modernity. As we do so, we may disagree a little more with each other, but that may be no bad thing if, at the same time, we seek to know Jesus a whole lot better and love each other a whole lot more than we have done in the past.

Embracing the mystery – humbly and wonderingly

All that we have said above is, I believe, true. We must enter the sanctuary to meet with God, we must tell the story of his self-revelation to us and we must do our theology to be true to what he has revealed. But it is incomplete. It will not be enough to take notes on the gist of the sermon; we must take note of the greatness of God. It will not be enough to understand the words of the preacher; we must stand in the presence of God. It will not be enough to be informed about the Bible; we must be inspired – literally 'in-breathed' – by the Spirit of God. It will not even be enough to be obedient to the authority of God, though we must never stop short of that. The ultimate purpose of worship and word is that we should bow before the majesty and mystery of a God who is ultimately and forever beyond our comprehension. It was Blaise Pascal who said, '*Le Dieu defini est le Dieu fini*'; a God who can be *defined* – apprehended by our intellects, held in our puny minds – is no longer God: merely a product of our thinking, a God made in our own image. And a God who is formed after our own image is no God at all.

Like Moses burdened by the task of bringing God's word to the people of Israel, the challenge of our times leaves us convinced that nothing else will distinguish us as the people of God unless God himself goes with us

(Ex 33: 12–23). Like Moses, the very promise of God's presence fills us with a longing to see him in all his glory. Like Moses, we must learn that we can never see him face to face on this earth. But, like Moses, we can find a place where the majesty and mystery of who God is passes before us, where we catch a glimpse of what can never be fully grasped, where we experience the wonder that can never be adequately explained in words: 'Then the Lord said, "There is a place near me where you may stand on a rock. When my glory passes by, I will put you in a cleft in the rock and cover you with my hand until I have passed by. Then I will remove my hand and you will see my back; but my face must not be seen"' (Ex. 33:21–23).

The preacher's calling in the Church and the Church's task in the world is to seek such intimacy with God and to speak with such simplicity and sincerity about our experience that others want to encounter him for themselves. For too long we have invited men and women to nothing better than a tame orthodoxy and a tedious conformity. It is time to draw them by the honesty of our words, by the reality of our works and, above all else, by the wonder that we carry within us, to a terrible beauty in which the hurts and sins of humanity are embraced by the healing and forgiveness of divinity. The awesome wonder of the crucified, risen Jesus, too magnificent for even the most eloquent words, can be adequately preached only and ultimately in the transformed lives of his followers.

I turn for an apt conclusion to this chapter to a writer whom one of my wisest and best friends described as 'the outrageous Annie Dillard'. To that description I would add the word 'courageous'. For she, as few others have done, has been brave enough to face the terrible beauty of a God who does not eliminate suffering from our world but who embraces and transforms it. He does it at Calvary and he does it all over again in the lives of those who walk with him. Annie Dillard's image of the traveller on the road is terrible and beautiful in equal measure. And it draws together the hurts we must encounter, the healing we can experience and the humanity that realises its destiny in the fierce splendour of gospel and grace.

> Divinity is not playful. The universe was not made in jest but in solemn incomprehensible earnest. By a power that is unfathomably secret and holy and fleet. There is nothing to be done about it, but ignore it, or see. And then you walk fearlessly, eating what you must, growing wherever you can, like the monk on the road who knows precisely how vulnerable he is, who takes no comfort among death-forgetting men and who carries his vision of vastness and might around in his tunic like a live coal which neither burns nor warms him, but with which he will not part.[17]

postscript

Poets and prophets have much in common. They see what the rest of us perceive only dimly and they say it with a strange, cold clarity that makes us wonder how we managed to miss it for so long. Then there's the fact that they turn up in unexpected places; you're just as likely to find them wandering in the streets and loitering in the market-place as sitting with the faithful in the sanctuary. And they have a disconcerting habit of being worryingly unorthodox but still managing to take us right to the heart of all that we profess to believe and practice; they're far more concerned about saying what's on their heart than they are about fitting in with the status quo. Sometimes, like the rest of humankind, they can be plain wrong in what they're telling us; they misunderstand the message or get the words all mixed up. But more often than we realise, from their position on the edge of things, they challenge us to an encounter with uncomfortable realities and unexpected truths.

Earlier in this book we recognised the profound insights of the poet-prophet Isaiah as he looked forward and dreamed of the One who would carry the pain and pay the penalty of a world in desperate need of grace.

But it seems to me that the prophetic voice continues to challenge us in our own generation, often from outside the Church. Despite the trivia of much that passes for entertainment, there is a persistent plea in contemporary novels and plays and movies, a persistent plea for the world to be touched and transformed by grace. Of course, they don't always – perhaps hardly ever – provide 'Christian answers'; but again and again they raise the right questions that challenge us to respond by living *grace-fully* and engaging meaningfully with our culture. Ian McEwan's magnificent novel, *Atonement*, for example, is the deeply moving tale of an author who spends a lifetime trying to re-write the story of her own life and those whose lives were fatally damaged by her thoughtless action in youth. Towards the end of the book, there is a poignant paragraph in which she sums up her dilemma

> The problem these fifty-nine years has been this: how can a novelist achieve atonement when, with her absolute power of deciding outcomes, she is also God? There is no-one, no entity or higher form that she can appeal to, or be reconciled with, or that can forgive her. There is nothing outside her. In her imagination she has set the limits and the terms. No atonement for God, or novelists, even if they are atheists. It was always an impossible task and that was precisely the point. The attempt was all.[18]

The Christian response is that we do not only write our own stories; rather, we are all part of a *greater* story – a story whose plot is full of complex twists and terrible sins, a story played out against the backdrop of the great, powerful movements of history. But it is a story that is shot through with grace, not an easy solution to every perplexing problem or a glib answer to every troubling question, but a fierce and terrible love in which the Author of all things takes upon himself the pain of his creation and makes atonement for every wrong and every injustice. It is a story whose pivotal moments and central scenes are all about a bloody cross and a broken grave. And it is a story that, if it is to be believed, must be fleshed out again in the life of every individual follower of Jesus and demonstrated by the transforming ministry of the Church in the world.

When Paul wrote his great letter to the Christians in Rome, he penned some sublime passages in which he was far more of a visionary poet than a systematic theologian. None is greater than that in which he looked forward to the completion of God's plan to redeem and renew his creation. In the mixture of joy and sorrow, pleasure and suffering, terror and beauty, faith and doubt that is the life of the believer and the calling of the Church, God is revealing his ultimate purpose through those who keep their promise and hold to their faith

> I consider that our present sufferings are not worth comparing to the glory that will be revealed in us. The creation waits in eager expectation for the sons of God to be revealed. For the creation was subjected to frustration, not by its own choice, but by the will of the one who subjected it, in hope that the creation itself will be liberated from its bondage to decay and brought into the glorious freedom of the children of God (Rom. 8:18–21).

Grace and gospel take us beyond merely hoping for the elimination of suffering; they lead us to the far more wonderful miracle of its transformation, the working out in every circumstance of the power of the cross, so that the crucifixion of hate and evil and pain become the opportunity for the resurrection of love and goodness and the power of God. That is the terrible beauty to which we are called. It is a costly calling, but those who hear and respond find it to be the best road to walk. And they discover that they make the journey in the company of the One who knows the route and who has already reached the destination.

endnotes

1. Isaac Watts (17 July 1674 – 25 November 1748) is recognised as the 'Father of English Hymnody'.
2. Williams, R., *A Ray of Darkness* (Cambridge, Mass: Cowley Productions, 1995).
3. Kempis, Thomas à, *The Imitation of Christ* (London: Penguin, 1973).
4. Yancey, P., *What's So Amazing About Grace?* (Grand Rapids: Zondervan, 1997).
5. Stuart Murray, *Post-Christendom: Church and Mission in a Strange New World* (Milton Keynes: Paternoster, 2004).
6. Schweitzer, A., *The Quest of the Historical Jesus* (London: A & C Black, 1910).
7. Martin, W., *With God on Our Side* (New York: Broadway Books, 1996).
8. Grenz, S., *Revisioning Evangelical Theology* (Illinois: IVP, 1993).
9. J B Phillips translation.
10. Barnes, C., *Words of William Booth* (London: S.P. & S., 1975).
11. Humphrys, J., *In God We Doubt* (London: Hodder & Stoughton, 2007).
12. Geldof, B., *Is That It?* (New York: Weidenfeld and Nicolson, 1986).

13 Doig, D., *Mother Teresa: Her People and Her Work* (Glasgow: Collins, 1976).

14 http://salt.claretianpubs.org/index.html Salt of the Earth, the social justice website for the Claretians.

15 Thielicke, H., *Encounter with Spurgeon* (London: James Clarke & Co, 1964).

16 McLaren, B., *The Church on the Other Side* (Grand Rapids: Zondervan, 1998).

17 Dillard, A., *Pilgrim at Tinker Creek* (New York: Harper Perennial, 1974).

18 McEwan, I. *Atonement* (London: Vintage books, 2007).